COURT
IN THE
MIDDLE

andrew fraser

COURT IN THE MIDDLE

Hardie Grant Books

Published in 2007
Hardie Grant Books
85 High Street
Prahran, Victoria 3181, Australia
www.hardiegrant.com.au

Cataloguing-in-Publication data is available from the National
Library of Australia.
Court in the middle
ISBN 978 1 7406 6555 1

Edited by Sally Moss
Cover design by Pat Sofra
Cover photograph by Jason Smith, The Age Photo Sales
Printed and bound in Australia by Trojan Press

10 9 8 7 6 5 4 3 2

Contents

For Lachlan and Olivia

The year's at the spring
And day's at the morn;
Morning's at seven;
The hillside's dew-pearled;
The lark's on the wing;
The snail's on the thorn;
God's in his heaven –
All's right with the world!
PIPPA'S PASSES, ROBERT BROWNING

Chapter One

Day In

*From the sublime to the ridiculous is
but one small step.*

ATTRIBUTED TO NAPOLEON BONAPARTE
ON HIS RETURN FROM HIS DISASTROUS
RUSSIAN CAMPAIGN IN 1812

Silence! All stand!

His Honour Judge Leo Hart crashes open the door from the judges' anteroom and, with head down, strides to his seat on the bench. Still not looking up, he opens the court and begins his sentencing of me and my co-accused.

At this point, one wonders how a lawyer like me, who for many years had a thriving practice both in Australia and overseas, has managed to plumb such depths as to end up standing in the dock of the County Court of the State of Victoria, Australia, to be sentenced for my part in being knowingly concerned with the importation of a commercial quantity of cocaine. I suppose the answer is simple and can be summed up in one word: addiction.

It is the very nature of addiction that drives you to indiscriminate behaviour, poor choices and, frankly, total disregard for the future consequences of your present actions. You merely barge onwards in the overriding desire to purchase and consume drugs. In my case, the drug was cocaine.

His Honour commences with a brief recitation of the facts: One Werner Roberts, a New Zealand national, together with his wife, Andrea Mohr, and a friend of theirs, Carl Urbanec, had conspired to import, and then actually imported, into Australia from Benin in East Africa eight ornamental plaques concealing a quantity of white powder. The white powder weighed 5.55 kilograms and contained 3.7 kilograms of pure cocaine valued at something between A$1.35 and A$2.7 million.

It strikes me as odd that supposed experts within the police force can only give such a wildly varying estimate. From what I have been told over the years, cocaine sold wholesale – which is what Roberts intended – was worth somewhere in the vicinity of $100,000 a kilo, making the total amount of imported white powder worth $555,000. I suppose it doesn't really matter now, but one must make these observations. No one has ever been able to adequately explain to me how courts continue to accept as fact the stratospheric figures placed by the police on virtually any drug deal.

Roberts was the importer and Mohr and Urbanec were

his supporters. As for my role, Roberts, Mohr and Urbanec as a group were my major cocaine suppliers and the Judge conceded that I only became involved in this escapade due to my addiction.

The Crown further alleged in its agreed statement of facts, and the Court found, that I was incidental to the importation, that the importation was already set in stone when Roberts had his conversation with me at my office and that it would have taken place whether I had been involved or not.

Apart from the obvious activity of me travelling backwards and forwards to Roberts's house to purchase cocaine on more occasions than you've had hot dinners, the only evidence alleged against me was the content of a conversation held in my office the night before Roberts departed for Benin.

You may well ask yourself: What is a solicitor's office doing being bugged by the Drug Squad? I will deal with that question later; suffice to say that it is a matter of corrupt police endeavouring to cover their own backsides. The fact that their own corrupt activities came to a screaming holt not long after I was jailed just goes to show that there is some justice in this world after all.

On the eve of Roberts's departure to Benin, he came to my office with some cocaine and we consumed the white powder along with some red wine. He told me what he had planned and that he intended to use an unwitting mule, Carol Brand, to actually bring in the plaques. Stupidly I said nothing about that plan and was foolish enough to give advice about going through customs. Roberts certainly didn't need this advice as, on his own admission, he had been a professional international drug dealer and smuggler for many years. The interesting part about all of this is that, according to what I was told, Roberts was actually working for Urbanec. And it was Mohr and Roberts who were the lieutenants to Urbanec. Urbanec's lawyers were clever enough to get him well and truly down the scale of things as far as his sentencing was concerned.

At this point I should say that this book is not meant to be a whinge about how hard done by I was. The reality of the matter is that I made a big mistake and I paid what could only be described as an overly hefty price for that mistake. That does not mean that I am happy with the treatment I received – treatment that involved corruption among police in the Victoria Police Drug Squad (which, by the way, has now been disbanded due to that corruption) and their conspiracy against me. And, yes, I am very unhappy with the learned (and I use that word advisedly) trial judge who gave me a sentence that was breathtaking in its size. This whole sad episode is behind me but I think people should know the truth about what happened in the case.

After my arrest, the four police who were involved in the team that investigated me – Detective Senior Sergeant Wayne Strawhorn, Detective Sergeant Malcolm Rozenes and Senior Detectives Paton and Firth – were all investigated for corruption, with the result that Strawhorn, Paton and Rozenes were all charged, convicted and sentenced to lengthy terms of imprisonment for their corrupt activities. It is an interesting observation that the sentences they received for their endemic corruption were far shorter than the sentence I received. Is the old adage true that coppers get less, when and if they are convicted? The answer seems to me to be an unequivocal yes. Firth was not charged but was suspended and left the police force under what could only be described as a substantial cloud, with question marks left hanging over the propriety of his behaviour and over his honesty.

What an interesting situation, then, with me already on bail charged with certain offences and these officers being the charging officers while they themselves are charged with corrupt activity but (at that stage) not yet convicted. It later came to light that both Rozenes and Paton, at the time of their arrest and before my sentencing, had both admitted their culpability and had made deals with the Ethical Standards section to give evidence if necessary.

His Honour would not allow the evidence of the police being charged to go before Roberts's jury when he pleaded not guilty – notwithstanding the fact that Roberts said that he carried out the importation only at the behest of Rozenes. The fact was never aired that Paton and Rozenes had already admitted their culpability during Roberts's trial. Why not? You may well ask.

Ethical Standards in turn have certain questions to

answer, due to their cherry picking approach to prosecuting corrupt police, playing corrupt coppers off one against the other in return for evidence and one corrupt police officer being allowed to get off Scot free in return for that evidence. Their refusal and/or failure to investigate allegations against other corrupt police and only concentrate on the scalps that will give them maximum publicity certainly bears closer examination.

All of these matters were racing through my mind as I sat in the dock on that fateful morning, 3 December, 2001.

As previously mentioned, His Honour did not look up at all while sentencing Roberts to thirteen years' imprisonment with a minimum of ten years. I didn't like the way this is going, with Roberts having just received a huge whack for the crime.

Next was Andrea Mohr, who was sentenced to a period of eight years but was granted a non-parole period of five. It is clear from the evidence that Mohr was the person who had the connection in Africa, who made contact with that connection, who arranged for Roberts to travel and who arranged the money for him to purchase the cocaine. If she got five years, surely I would get a stack less, bearing in mind that the Crown had conceded that I was incidental to the importation and that it was set in stone before I had my conversation with Roberts.

Urbanec was the third to be sentenced; he got nine

years. I couldn't believe this because, on any assessment, the evidence before the court painted him as a gofer at best. Yet he received a minimum of six years on the bottom.

I still held out hope that my sentence, or part of my sentence, could be wholly or partially suspended. I was about to learn the first lesson of being in jail.

Coming up from the holding cells that morning I had been talking to a prison officer who told me that the consensus among the screws was that I would receive a smack on the hand and, as they say in the vernacular, "sign the sorry book" and go home. The reason, they believed, that I had already spent a couple of weeks in custody since the plea awaiting sentence was that His Honour wanted to scare the living Jesus out of me. If that was His Honour's rationale, then mission accomplished. But the lesson I had to learn was never, under any circumstances, believe the assessment of a prison officer. In my experience, they are always – yes, always, without exception – wrong. Talk about empty vessels making the most noise!

Trying to view what was happening to me as dispassionately as a lawyer should just didn't work. I was petrified as I heard the words being said to me: "Prisoner Fraser, stand up."

The change in His Honour's demeanour was dramatic. While sentencing Roberts, Mohr and Urbanec, he had kept his head down and effectively appeared to be a small target. When it came to me, His Honour physically lifted himself up, stuck out his chest and eyeballed me as he gave it to me in no uncertain terms. It is clear from reading the sentence that I was sentenced for who I was not what I had done. In other words, the fact that I had been a lawyer and got myself an addiction, had been a lawyer and become involved – no matter how peripherally – in this importation, had been a lawyer and allowed myself to plumb the depths I had, demanded what was requisite of condign punishment. I can remember standing in the dock gripping the rail at the front, thinking to myself, if I let go here I will fall down and I am not going to give this bastard the satisfaction of seeing that happen – nor, for that matter, Strawhorn and all his cronies sitting in the front row of the court.

His Honour then sentenced me to a maximum of seven years with a minimum of five. Never in my life have I received such a dreadful shock, been so stunned or so frightened. As a criminal lawyer, practising across this country and doing numerous cases around the world, I have been in virtually every jail in Australia and I reckon I know a bit about the game. Yet nothing could possibly have prepared me for what would follow.

I was struck dumb. I looked up at my mother and my wife; they were in tears. I was too stunned to move. Before His Honour could even leave the Court, two prison officers came into the court, opened the dock, grabbed me and hauled me out unceremoniously. That was the end of my life as I had known it up until that date.

Even when I'd been charged, even when I had had my committal and after the rubbish that Tim Watson-Munro had said at my committal, I was still of the opinion – naively, perhaps, like a drowning man clutching at straws – that the truth of this matter would come out and everything would be alright. Yes, I would probably get a jail sentence, but it wouldn't be a big one. Stupidly I still had faith in the system that I had worked in for twenty-eight years. I was sadly mistaken: I had underestimated the cruelty of the system when the axe falls on one of its own.

If I had, for instance, been a doctor of medicine with such a habit, first up I would have received substantial treatment from another doctor at the behest of the peak body the Australian Medical Association. And then that treatment would have been ongoing, together with peer support to help me through my crisis. For lawyers, there was (and still is) no such counselling and certainly no such support.

As soon as I was arrested, application was made to strike me off the roll as a practising lawyer and I was audited twice. The coppers were sure that I had stuck the contents of my trust account up my nose, so they very unhappy when they grabbed all my trust account records and had them audited only to find that the trust account was intact to the cent and balanced exactly. They were so pissed off that I was audited again a couple of weeks later. Same result. Yes, I had been stupid, in that I had stuck my own superannuation up my nose; but, no, I had not touched my trust account to feed my habit. Of course, if I had used my trust account to continue my habit, that would have been a dreadful aggravating circumstance in my case and I would have received a much longer sentence. Lucky I had some brains left, notwithstanding the rampant addiction I was suffering.

Dragged out of court on my own, I was separated from my co-accused and taken down in the lift to the holding cell where I was pushed in and then heard the most chilling sound anyone could ever hear in their life: the sound of a steel door slamming behind me and the key being turned. You are in the nick now, son, and you have blown your entire life.

I cannot – even now, writing this book – begin to describe the feeling of total desolation, of hopelessness and of fear of the great unknown. And, boy, was I ever about to take a trip into the great unknown! Luckily I was able to survive it and live to tell the tale. But the person writing this book today is a totally different person from the one who went to prison back in November 2001. Some of life's lessons are hard learnt; was this ever a hard-learnt lesson on many fronts!

As I was being led from the court I remember looking straight ahead. The only thing I could see in front of me was Detective Senior Sergeant Wayne Strawhorn. He was standing there smiling at me and receiving congratulatory handshakes from all his copper mates. I knew what Strawhorn had been up to and I knew that he was corrupt. I further knew that the genesis of my prosecution was Strawhorn's attempt to deflect an investigation from him and he had been successful.

I wondered whether he would ever get his right whack for his corrupt activities. Luckily, I am pleased to announce that, in the long run, he was brought undone. As I write this book, I am out, I am rehabilitated, I am drug free and I am building a new life. Wayne Strawhorn is still in jail, a disgraced corrupt copper. If Ethical Standards bother to properly investigate Wayne Strawhorn and the other officers who were involved in the Victorian Drug Squad, one hell of a viper's nest will be uncovered. I am convinced that is the reason why the Ethical Standards division have refused to act on my complaints, but that's another matter.

I was told that a friend of mine who was a lawyer got in the lift with Strawhorn and other coppers after the sentencing and they were cock'a'hoop at my imprisonment. My mate was disgusted at what was being said.

It was a big night at Goldfingers "gentleman's" club in King Street, Melbourne, that night. For those of you who don't know, Goldfingers is tabletop dancing establishment whose owner has close links to the police – obviously the right place for the drug boys to celebrate the fact that they had just effectively slaughtered somebody who had been a pain in their neck for many years. I know where all of this animosity started and I'll deal with that later in the book; but for the time being I was sitting in a holding cell in the bowels of the County Court in Melbourne pondering my fate. Frankly I didn't know whether to sit, stand, cry, vomit or what, but I could not have hung myself because at that stage my belt, my tie and my shoelaces had been taken away from me as a precaution against self-harm.

I don't know what I would have done if I'd had the means to hang myself but I doubt very much that I would have committed suicide. Contrary to popular belief, whereby it is said that only gutless people kill themselves, I actually hold a different view after all that I've seen in jail. I think if you suicide you are in fact a far braver person that those who criticise and frankly I didn't have the guts to kill myself. In any event, suicide is a bit permanent for my liking; from my observations over the years, it's a bit hard to change your mind once you're dead!

One of the hardest things for a lawyer who has just received a shitty result for their client is to take that long ride down in the lift to the holding cells under the court and face up to the punter. Invariably you say "Well, that was a bad result. We'll have to appeal and see if we can't do better on appeal." The reality is, once you have received a large sentence in the first instance in Australia, getting anywhere on appeal is a bit like the bloke with the wheelbarrow: you've got the job in front of you! Anyway I didn't have to worry about any of that because my counsel didn't come and see me afterwards. I did notice on the television news that night that he said he was dumbfounded by the sentence and we would appeal. Thank you for stating the bleeding obvious.

A very good mate of mine who was in another court and had been a constant support to me all through this. Dr Greg

Lyon SC had heard about my sentence as it had travelled through the court system like wildfire because of my profile and the types of cases I'd been doing over the years. He came down and saw me and said he couldn't believe the sentence I had received.

In fact, the sentence was so far above what anybody expected that I half anticipated the Crown might, for once, do the honourable thing and concede an appeal – that is, concede that my sentence should be reduced on the grounds that the sentence imposed was manifestly excessive. This was not merely wishful thinking: there had been numerous discussions backwards and forwards between my counsel and Richard Maidment, the counsel for the Commonwealth, and it had been agreed that, if I received less than a year (not seven years), then the Crown would appeal. I wonder what exercised Mr Maidment's mind following the result that I received from Judge Heart because, on appeal in the Supreme Court, he certainly didn't say he reckoned I got too much, even though he had told my counsel that he was dumbfounded at the result.

Sitting in the holding cell, I saw my life flash before me. The first thought was for my family: my poor wife, whom I had put through so much; my little kids, who were still young, wouldn't have a dad for a long period of time. They were the people I was concerned for. Yes, I was apprehensive – not scared for myself, because I didn't know what was coming around the corner for me, but concerned for my family, their well being. I had not left them properly provided for because, frankly, after I was arrested, I lost the plot.

I got off the drugs – and boy was that a struggle – but then I started drinking too much. Obviously, looking at it in retrospect, the drinking was just a replacement for the drug use. Add to that the pressure of the prosecution, the constant media coverage, speculation surrounding my case and the Law Institute of Victoria applying to have my practising certificate cancelled, and I was almost a basket case by the time the matter got to court.

Looking back, I'm rather surprised that I was able to hold myself together. Now that I was sentenced, it had all hit the wall in one hell of a splat. There was now no hope, there was now no speculation as to how this case would go, there was now no speculation as to whether I would receive a suspended sentence. I was in jail and I was looking down the barrel of a big whack and I had to come to terms with it. What I know now is that if you put one foot in front of the other, you can usually get through most things in life.

I was asked if I wanted a sandwich for lunch and a cup of tea. I could only manage a cup of tea and that was the beginning of a rather severe diet and change in myself. I think I was probably in shock for a good two years over the sentence I received. I certainly suffered depression – a condition that I used to think was imagined – and I began to suffer (and still occasionally suffer) panic attacks, another malady that I used to consider a fallacy. It's a bit like having a cross between a heart attack and an asthma attack. Try having a panic attack when you are locked in a prison cell! When you call for help you are told to "Fuck off". The only thing you can do is hang on for dear life and hope to Christ that morning is not far away. I do not recommend it.

I was told I was going to be moved quickly and taken to Melbourne Assessment Prison (MAP) in Spencer Street, where I would be held until they decided what to do with me. Melbourne Assessment Prison is a relatively new prison, not quite twenty years old, on the fringe of the central business district of Melbourne. It's where prisoners are held while on remand and prisoners serving long sentences are held for short periods if they need medical treatment or are insane.

At the time I was dumbfounded by the number of mentally ill people in the prison system. One wonders what in God's name they are doing in a prison when, in fact, they should be in proper facilities for the mentally infirm. But the governments of today, in their wisdom, consider the bottom line economically more important than the welfare of mentally ill people, who are merely another statistic.

MAP is poorly run. Apart from a gymnasium, there are no exercise facilities and there is absolutely no rehabilitation or support for any prisoner suffering as a result of being sentenced or locked up.

I didn't know it at the time, but I was placed on suicide watch. That first night in jail the trap in my cell door was being opened every hour and a torch being shone in.

Needless to say, this scared the living daylights out of me each time because I was not expecting it and, of course, in the middle of the night one's imagination runs riot – I thought that on each occasion that some dreadful mischief was about to be visited on me. Luckily, not so.

I was taken to meet the jail governor, whose language shocked me. I should point out that if you were to take the words fuck, cunt, goose and imbecile out of the prison lexicon then you would be able to hear a pin drop. Unfortunately that applies equally to most of the screws, who seem to think it's clever or necessary to address you in that manner. I did my very best not to fall into the same trap, but that is very difficult when it's all you hear day in, day out. Anyway, by the time the Governor had finished his "fuck this, fuck that" tirade to me about now being in fucking jail and I'd better fucking well get used to it, and if I don't like it, well then don't come to fucking jail, I was put in the protection unit away from all the other remand prisoners. Under protection, you're in with the paedophiles, the child killers, the laggers (who have told so many stories that everybody else in the system wants to kill them) and other people who just didn't have the guts to stay in the prison mainstream because of what they may or may not have seen or done in the past.

Notwithstanding the fact that I'd been a lawyer, I had no idea (and was never told) that you were supposed to ask to be placed in protection – it couldn't be forced on you – and you had to sign a protection request form to confirm this. I never signed any such form and I only found out by accident a couple of years into my sentence that I could demand to be removed from protection to mainstream, which duly occurred.

The first thing you notice when you go to jail is that you are given no instructions whatsoever as to jail procedures and regulations. You are left in blissful ignorance as to what is required of you, as though you are expected to learn by osmosis. When you are about to be released you are given a book entitled Getting Out; why aren't you given similar instructions on going in? No doubt it's because you are easier to control if you are kept in the dark.

I had come to MAP late in the day, after lockdown. All the prisoners are locked down in their cells each day from 4.30 pm until 8.30 am the next morning. It is not a good existence. I was taken upstairs to the protection unit in the security lift surrounded by screws as if I was Ivan Milat. I couldn't believe the treatment I was receiving. I was taken to my cell, the door was opened and I was ushered in. On a bench in the cell was a cold plate of what was supposed to be food and the door was slammed behind me. Yet again a chill ran down my back as I heard the sound of steel slamming on steel and a heavy key turning in a heavy lock. It takes a special kind of person to turn the key and lock up another human being. Despite all the claims made by prison officers about how good the pay is and how good the conditions are, or any other piece of nonsense they want to utter as a reason for choosing their job, the reality is that you must – I repeat: you must – have some sort of sadistic streak in you to want to be a prison officer.

The unit was small. It held just over twenty men, about half in single cells and the rest in doubles. I was lucky enough to get a single cell straight off. I didn't know who I was in with until the next morning. I sat on the bed, which was a plastic-coated piece of foam similar to a camp stretcher mattress; to say that it looked uncomfortable and uninviting is an understatement. There were two rough army-type blankets and two putrid pillows without pillowslips, together with one towel. My first and overwhelming memory of that cell was the stench of stale urine.

The next morning, as soon as I could, I obtained some cleaning materials and tried to clean the cell – to no avail. It had clearly been inhabited by people who had lost all self-esteem and the human waste had permeated the floor and the walls. That stench would pervade my life for the next few months. The other overwhelming memory is of how dirty everything was. There was a cup and a plate and a knife and fork. They seemed to have had little more than a cursory rinse for a very long time: the cup was caked, inside and out, with a residue of instant coffee and sugar. I didn't touch anything that night. I didn't even have a drink of water from the tiny stainless steel sink bolted to the wall because it was so dirty and I was conscious of bacteria. That was the start of my regime of fastidiousness. Every time I went into a new cell, the first thing I would do was obtain cleaning materials and scrub it from ceiling to floor – literally – and then flush it out as best I could. Then, every time I went outside my cell and returned to it, I immediately washed my hands. I think that helped me stay relatively well, at least physically, during my period of incarceration.

There was a TV in the cell – a small battered set with no clear reception on any channel. The excuse given was that all of the internal security systems within the prison interfered with reception. I didn't accept that for a moment; clearly the quality of the sets was due to a combination of cost cutting, laziness and the old adage that there are no votes in prisoners.

I hope you can get some idea of my total desolation at this stage. I sat on the end of my bed still in my suit pants and shirt (no clothes were provided; I had to wait for my wife to drop in a tracksuit) and I wondered what came next. There was a window, which was barred and then had Perspex on the inside so that there were no hanging points. I looked around the rest of the cell: no hanging points anywhere. Not that killing myself was an option for me. However, I soon found out that where there is a will, there is a way: suicide is an exit that a number of people take when faced with the hopelessness of a jail sentence. It didn't take long for me to work out that there are three options when you are sentenced: you either sit in the corner and cry, which a lot of blokes do; you neck yourself, which some do as well; or you get on with it – as the crooks say, kick along with it, do the best you can.

MAP, unlike the others prisons in which I served my sentence, is a remand-only prison so is not obliged to provide any of the structure normally found in a prison. There are no activities and all the jail provides is food, which you do not necessarily receive; it is not obliged to provide clothes or any other item for your general wellbeing.

There is a canteen selling a few items, which you can access once a week. Your cell cannot be locked from the inside and once the cell is unlocked by the screws in the morning, it stays that way until they lock it again at 4.30 each afternoon. You can imagine the amount of petty thieving that goes on in such an environment. It was here that I first witnessed prisoners carrying out their own summary justice. As already mentioned, the cell doors are steel. They are big, they are heavy and they are locked into a steel frame. A bloke was caught thieving from another cell by a couple of old hands who were on remand for rather serious offences. They grabbed hold of the perpetrator's hand, held it against the door frame and slammed the steel door hard on it. You cannot begin to imagine the sound of that man's screaming as his mangled hand was removed from the door frame. I sincerely doubt whether his hand would ever be useful again.

The screws knew that this was happening as it was obvious, yet nothing was done until after the punishment had been carried out. It was then that the screws made their move and the perpetrators were subsequently charged with the disciplinary offence. This was where I learnt "jail law"

– namely, that of the three wise monkeys. You see no evil, you hear no evil and you speak no evil. If you see something going on, even if you disagree with it vehemently, it is not worth your own personal safety or wellbeing to stick your bib in and get involved. The repercussions to you could well be profound and you'd probably get no thanks from the bloke you tried to help anyway. Jail is quite literally every man for himself – and for me, having spent a large proportion of my life trying to help other people by appearing for them, this was a very difficult situation to accept.

Because of the type of place that MAP was, feelings tended to run high. Everybody was on remand; because they had not had their cases dealt with they were all under pressure and justifiably edgy. This, of course, brought about constant arguments between people. Fear of the unknown affected everybody, not just me. This was a real pressure cooker environment and you could see when things were going to happen and if I could see it, as somebody who had been in jail for five minutes, surely the screws could see it as well. After all, aren't they the people who are supposed to be professionals and understand what precisely is going on and hopefully be able to stamp it out in advance? I think not.

It wasn't long before I had learnt jail lesson number two: do not stand in the food queue. The reason? That is where you get jumped. As I said, everybody is edgy, anxious, uptight – and in such an atmosphere blow-ups occur very easily. On any given day, just standing in the food queue, somebody would get belted or stabbed from behind. You may well ask how people come to have stabbing implements in a maximum-security, small, controlled environment. The answer is that virtually everything is a weapon if you want it to be.

The powers that be in the jail were obsessed with weapons. I was not allowed a hardback book in MAP because either it could be used as a weapon or the cover could contain drugs. A book as a weapon I can understand, as the pen is mightier than the sword. But the irony was that we were all allowed to have pens and pencils! A sharp pencil makes a very good stabbing implement and I have seen them used in that manner. The other favourite jail weapon was a toothbrush with the head broken off. The broken end of the toothbrush was then sharpened to a point on the concrete floor. A little bit of rag around one end to make a handle, and you had a very handy stabbing implement that could inflict serious damage in a very short period of time. I have seen blokes stand behind others in the food queue, the hand goes down the front of the tracksuit pants and in the blink of an eye out comes the toothbrush: bang, bang, bang. Three or four stabs in the back, neck and head, and then it is on for young and old. You didn't need to actually offend someone to have this happen to you: a perceived slight was sufficient to result in retribution of the most violent nature.

So, on the days when I could bring myself to eat, which was not all that often, I would wait until the food queue had subsided. If that meant missing out on my lunch or my dinner, so be it; better to go hungry than to end up with a pencil hanging out of my jugular vein.

As a lawyer, I had always been extremely busy, my days filled with running from courts to clients, jumping on and off planes and generally not having time to scratch myself. In a stride I went from that existence to one where each day on the inside dragged like a year on the outside. This feeling of time standing still was highlighted and aggravated by the fact that MAP is in the city centre and I could see out my window to the world that I once knew. I would sit for hours at a time just staring out the window.

The only highlight of the day was the one hour when we were taken down to the gym. The track at the gym was 80 metres around, and I was so unfit when I went to jail that I couldn't run ten laps of it. This was somebody who was a pretty fair athlete in his day and had competed at high levels for many years in the 400 metre hurdles. There was only one thing to do: make myself as tired as possible during that exercise time, in the hope that I might get some sleep that night. It did work occasionally but every night for many years, at 3.35 am or thereabouts, I would sit bolt upright sweating profusely, my heart pounding in my chest... Shit, where am I? What's going on? What has happened? Then I would realise that I was in jail. Why 3.35 am? That was precisely the time when the police ran through the door at my house and arrested me, thus bringing about the beginning of the end of my former life. It took many years for this habit to subside and when it finally did, it almost seemed strange that I was able to go a complete night without this shocking interruption.

I remember how, on the first morning, when the cell door was unlocked, I thought: This is it, here we go. When the door was flung open, I stayed seated at my bench, looking at the wall. By the time I turned to leave my cell, there was a large man standing in the doorway. He was clearly off his face, even though it was only 8.30 am. "Who the fuck are you?" he said in a belligerent manner. My guts tightened. I told him. He stopped, smiled, walked over and shook my hand, introducing himself. "You acted for my old man for years. He told me to look out for you. Good, stick with me, you'll be right." That was a relief and a half, I can tell you. But the fact that the door, once unlocked, couldn't be snibbed again from the inside was a worry because a lot of blokes had summary justice handed out to them by other prisoners going into their cells and assaulting them for no apparent reason.

I then emerged from my cell to see the brother of another one of my clients who was in protection because he had told on some very heavy people and his wellbeing could not be assured if he was in the mainstream. He was a huge man covered in tattoos but had a reputation as a serial lagger (police informer).

These were the people I was to live with for the next few months. They did, however, show me how to at least get started in jail – namely to get some more bedding if I needed it, get a cleaner pillow, and so on (all of which, by the way, the screws would then take away from you the next day because you had more than your issue allowed). I know these things sound infinitesimal in the context of a normal every-day existence but in jail they assume enormous importance. There is a certain amount of satisfaction in being able to get yourself something that other blokes can't get.

One of the old lags suggested that I should try to get a prison job immediately: it would give me a little bit of money and would help pass the time. When I received my first pay slip in jail, I realised that it would take me three months to earn what I used to charge per hour. Try that for a reality check!

I was employed doing general duties in the Acute Assessment Unit – or AAU – which was where all the blokes who are stark raving insane are housed. The AAU was on the top floor of MAP, with one small exercise yard which was probably eight metres by six metres. It was chock-a-block due to the mental health system in this state being gutted by the government in the name of economic rationalism, as already mentioned. What we have been left with is a jail system full of mentally ill people who should be in psychiatric institutions, not jails. Nobody seems to care until somebody gets out and re-offends; then of course, there's a huge squawk about it. Why wasn't something done? Where in God's name is the rehabilitation? Well, the answer to those questions is quite simple. If you want nothing done, that's exactly what will happen: nothing. Until somebody gets their head around the fact that most prisoners will eventually be released from jail, so they will need to be properly monitored and rehabilitated. Until then, it is our society as a general proposition that is the sufferer, not individuals.

The AAU was a real eye opener for me. The blokes in there had nowhere else to go. They were men who had been sent to the units for the insane to spend their sentences there but couldn't be contained because of their mental problems. Probably the best example of the shocking conditions that these men endured was Big Dino, who had, by the time I first met him, done about thirteen years for murder. He was not the full tin of biscuits and had done the entire thirteen years in maximum security. I would go to the AAU in the morning to clean up from the night before and he would be sitting somewhere staring at the wall. When I would go back later in the afternoon to feed them he would be sitting staring at the same wall. This man was so conditioned to jail that, when I was with him again at Port Phillip Prison, he would stand like Pavlov's dog at the servery which had a roller door in front of it, waiting for his food at a given time. This man, in his forties, couldn't even fill out his canteen form and couldn't roll his own smokes due to the amount of medication he was on. He was a self-mutilator who once cut his own penis off. It was sewn back on. His logic was "I'll fix them this time", so he cut it off again and swallowed it! If ever there was anyone who needed intense, one-on-one rehabilitation and counselling it was Dino – and he didn't get it.

That man has now been paroled, after fifteen years, and he is worse by a mile than he was when he went to jail. He was allowed to go and live with his grandmother, who was, if my memory serves me correctly, an old lady in her eighties. He was incapable of looking after himself to any degree.

Dino was epileptic but the genius who was the medical officer took him off his epileptic medication. He was at the top of some stairs at Port Phillip when he fell down in a severe grand mal fit. I lifted his head up and that was all I could do. He was a huge man. There was no good trying to subdue him or trying to hold him still.

How he coped when he left prison, I can only begin to guess. The real question is what was done for him during the time he was incarcerated. Yes, he was in for murder. Yes, it was bad murder as murders go – not that there are many good ones – but there was a substantial and severe mental impairment suffered by this man and to release him on parole at the end of fifteen years after having offered him no real help at all left me speechless. Dino was by no means the only bloke in that sort of situation in prison but he was one case that I had quite a lot to do with as he ended up being in the same unit as me at Port Phillip.

I served the meals at the AAU, which was quite an experience in itself. There were always about six screws standing around while the meal was being served, just in case anyone started to play up and of course they regularly did, with blokes upending their meals, chucking stuff at the screws, fighting each other in the queue. When I look back now, it seems almost laughable, if it weren't so bloody serious, that people who are this mad were going to be released at some stage into society.

The only benefit attached to working in the AAU was that I was given sachets of instant coffee and any leftover food to take back to my cell. Small consolation for the fact that I had to scrub the shit off the walls from the madmen who had "bronzed" their cells, which was a regular occurrence. Bronzing was new to me, but it is a very real protest in jail and particularly indulged in by those that aren't playing with a full deck. It didn't matter who you were, if you were the billet for the AAU, you cleaned this off the walls – end of story.

In the AAU I witnessed substantial violence towards the inmates because a lot of them, obviously not being all that well mentally, would play up and refuse to move or refuse to come out for their medication or refuse to see the doctor. Half a dozen screws would go into the cell and there would be hell to pay as a fight started. The inevitable outcome was that the -prisoner would lose, ending up well and truly the worse for wear. Whatever had to be done was done and then he was left for dead in his cell. By the way, these cells were absolutely disgraceful. What is the value of being human when virtually no other animal is required to eat, sleep, piss, shower and live all in the one space? If it is done to a battery hen, there is a hue and cry that would raise the roof, but because these are only crooks in our society, then that's OK. And where is the Commissioner for Corrections Victoria, Mr Kelvin Anderson, who sets the standards in these places, when the bashings are going on?

When one bloke was moved from the AAU to another jail, as the billet I had to clean the cell. This man had been allowed to live in a pigsty. It was filth from the ceiling all the way down the walls. The floor was caked with dirt, excrement and urine. Neither the hand basin nor the toilet had been cleaned and the shower was a disgrace. And it was my job to clean the lot. You are given rubber gloves and a bucket and a mop – a scrubbing brush is viewed as a luxury – and you do the best you can with these rudimentary cleaning items. Of course, everything is watered down in jail: the disinfectant is watered down, the detergent is watered down. Nothing works properly. It's all to do with saving a buck rather than getting things clean. I spent the best part of half a day trying to clean the small cell to some degree – but it was a losing battle, given that the cell seemed not to have been cleaned properly since the jail had been built. At the end of my efforts the screw had a look in and said "Yep, that'll do", then told me to fuck off. This was the usual form of exchange between screw and prisoner but I was determined that, no matter how often I was spoken to like that, I was not going to give the screws an opportunity to lay any charges against me. So I refused to yell back at them. I refused to swear at them and I refused to abuse them. Over the years I probably aggravated them more than prisoners who abused them constantly.

If I asked a question that they couldn't answer, the inevit-able retort was also "Fuck off." My reply to that was "No, I'm entitled to an answer and I would like one. I have a very long sentence with nothing else to do during that sentence, so I will sit here and wait until I get an answer." This usu-ally resulted in my being told to go to my cell or I would be charged with an offence against the good order and manage-ment of the jail. Now, if you can tell me what good order and management of the jail have to do with asking a question that they refuse to answer, I'll be amazed. But it is the one charge that it is virtually impossible to beat if the screws hit you with it. The screws used to laugh openly, saying "Oh well, if so-and-so doesn't behave himself'" – or gets too cheeky or won't do up his shoes or whatever else may take their fancy at the time – "we'll charge him with breaching good order and management of the jail and it is an iron-clad certainty that he will be convicted of the offence."

MAP, being a government jail, suffered far more violence from the screws than the other jails I was in. The other two – Port Phillip and Fulham (near Sale in Victoria) – were pri-vately run jails, which seemed to reduce the violence. One night on muster (a procedure where you are counted four times per day to make sure you are still there – "Muster up, stand by your open cell doors, no talking, no smoking, no farting; Muster up!" – and most times the count is wrong and a recount is called; after all, it is bloody hard to count 1 plus 1 plus 1), a young bloke back-chatted one of the screws. Without warning the screw turned around, grabbed him by the throat, smashed his head against the wall and then punched him in the face a number of times until he dropped to the floor. I had not seen this sort of gratuitous violence before in my life and it had quite a profound impact on me. This was a kid who was in his twenties, and he was just a smart-arse and a loudmouth. He didn't deserve that. I asked some of the crooks what usually happened in such a situation and they said "Absolutely nothing." It's no good making a complaint about it or saying anything to anybody because firstly nothing will get done about it and secondly you will then be branded a troublemaker and in turn invite trouble for yourself. So nothing is done about it and it becomes a self-fulfilling prophecy: you go to jail, you will be subjected to violence by officers and nothing will be done about it, and if you complain the screws will get you anyway and so it goes around and around and around ad infinitum. The circle of violence.

I really didn't make any friends at MAP. I was still too shocked. The experience of being in jail was something I simply could not accept, and my feeling of sheer helplessness was overwhelming. I'd gone from running my own practice and making all my own decisions to being banged up in prison: told what to eat, when to eat, when to get up, when to go to sleep, when to smile, when not to smile – all at the behest of an ignorant pig of a prison officer. The one observation I made repeatedly throughout my sentence was that the more ignorant the officer, the more they delighted in making my life in jail as uncomfortable as humanly possible.

I had gone into custody on the thirteenth of November and was sentenced on the third of December. Therefore Christmas was just around the corner. My first Christmas in jail was dreadful. I can't describe how bad I felt on that day. As far as I was concerned, the only way I could survive these sorts of occasions was for them not to exist in my mind, from that point on I ignored birthdays, Christmases or any other normal celebration that people in society celebrate as a matter of course. I was able to ring my family a couple of times on Christmas day for the allowable ten-minute conversation and that was it. No visitors Christmas day, and the food was still shit.

During the first long days of being locked down in my cell from 4.30 to 8.30, the enormity of what had happened to me started to sink in. It's during this time, when you sit and think, that you worry that this is a sentence you will never survive. Five years is so long, you can see no end. There is no hope, there is no light at the end of the tunnel. There isn't even a tunnel yet. And I started to dwell on my past and how I had come to be in such a sorry state.

Chapter 2
The Making of a Lawyer

The first thing we do, let's kill all the lawyers!
HENRY VI PART II, WILLIAM SHAKESPEARE

Every kid gets asked "What do you want to be when you grow up?" My answer from as far back as I can remember was always "I want to be a lawyer, I want to be a criminal lawyer, I want to be a criminal defence lawyer." I'm not sure exactly what it was that attracted me so strongly to criminal law, but a criminal defence lawyer was all I had ever wanted to be.

I think it started with my grandfather who, as a returned veteran of the Somme, always thought the ordinary bloke should have someone to stick up for him. This attitude lasted his entire life and was a profound and positive influence on me. As a lawyer himself, Grandpa had defended Jehovah's Witnesses who for religious reasons had allowed a child to die by refusing a blood transfusion. His attitude was that those people were entitled to their beliefs, even though he disagreed with them. Later he resigned from the RSL in protest when they voted to exclude communists from membership. Grandpa's attitude was that the sole criterion for RSL membership was that you were a returned serviceman and politics had no place in determining eligibility for membership. He resigned and walked out in front of a meeting of hundreds of blokes, never to return.

That is called sticking up for what you believe, and that attitude was drummed into me by my parents and the family generally. Everybody deserved a fair go in this country – that is what returned servicemen had fought for. A healthy scepticism of authority generally pervaded most discussions in our family and all the kids, no matter how young, were encouraged to voice their opinion. Once you had had your say, you had to be prepared to defend your position against any opposing view that may be aired – and there were plenty. Family dinner time was usually a robust affair, with lots of healthy and heated debate for all!

I come from a conservative family background where the emphasis was on academic and sporting achievement, and the family is full of lawyers. In addition to my mother's father, my maternal uncle, who has stuck by me through thick and thin, was a lawyer. My sister and brother-in-law are lawyers.

I'm not going to rattle on about my childhood, save to say that it was a happy and healthy one, I always felt safe and loved, and I was given every opportunity to achieve whatever I wished. My parents' view was: We are not going force any profession on you; all we ask is that, whatever you do, you be the best at it that you can possibly be. It followed that I wanted to be as good a criminal lawyer as I could possibly be.

I had a good education and I enjoyed debating at school. When I finished school I got into Law by just one mark. My course was at the Royal Melbourne Institute of Technology (RMIT). It was an articled clerks' course, which meant that, in place of five years' study at university, I did one year's full-time study, then spent four years working in a firm of solicitors, with lectures and tutorials before and after office hours and at lunch times. On reflection, this was best for me because if I'd gone to university, where you are allowed lots of spare time to study, I would not have made optimum use of that time. I'm the sort of bloke who, given free rein, will sit and procrastinate; I perform best under pressure.

I loved being articled. I loved the firm I was articled to, Haines Blakie and Polites, and I particularly liked the principal of the firm, Ken Haines. He was a no-bullshit old digger from the bush and he taught me many valuable lessons. A lot of people didn't like him because he was coarse and abrupt; but he knew the law and he was prepared to stick up for you if you were having a go and you could justify yourself to him.

In those days – the early 1970s – articled clerks were tantamount to slave labour. I remember that my first pay packet was something like $19 a week. That was less than half of what the most junior girl received because, in those days, there was no award for articled clerks. It was considered that you were of no real commercial benefit to a firm and that they were doing you a favour by employing you. You were there to learn and the cost of that was borne by the firm. Therefore, in my own practice, I always made a point of having at least one articled clerk at any given time because I considered it my obligation to the profession. I had been lucky enough to be given articles and that gave me my start in the law; in return I considered it was my obligation to do the same for the next generation of young lawyers. And I have had some terrific young lawyers work for me over the years, all full of enthusiasm and a couple in particular who went on to big things and have become successful partners in large firms. I must say I am rather proud of the latter when I still see them.

Life at Haines Blakie and Polites was all rough and tumble. The firm has since been reincarnated, but the type of practice it was – namely, a central city general practice – no longer exists. We did a bit of everything, and I was in general litigation. Litigation has some of the free-for-all component that's associated with the criminal law but not to the same degree, nor with the extreme consequences that are attached to the loss of a criminal case.

It was there that I got a real taste for being in court, seeing barristers appearing in personal injuries cases, car accident cases or building cases. That's where I had a great deal of contact with clients, as well as other barristers and solicitors, and I thoroughly enjoyed my time doing that sort of work.

Being a central city practice and a general practice, there was always a little bit of crime – whether it was a company director's wife who had succumbed to menopause and committed shop lifting, somebody's son who'd pinched a car or belted a copper, or even the occasional serious charge such as culpable driving or manslaughter.

The firm had had a substantial presence in the Kaye abortion enquiry back in the late 1960s and early 1970s and a number of prosecutions flowed from that as well. I busted my boiler to work or help out in whatever way I could in those cases. The more I got involved, the more it confirmed for me that this was what I really wanted to do with my professional life: I wanted to be a criminal lawyer.

In 1975 I was admitted to practice and the partners sat me down and asked me what I saw as my future. I told them I wanted to capitalise on the small amount of crime that came through the door and build a criminal practice for the firm. Ken Haines was smart enough to see the logic in this, and that it would be another string to the firm's bow, so I was given the go-ahead to try and build that practice.

I vividly recall how we had one client by the name of Brian Donald Latch, or Brian Donald Gardiner, who had been famous for the Mr X police enquiry back in the 1960s. He was a petty thief who continually got himself into bother. He had a string of kids, most of whom were also getting themselves into constant bother. One in particular, Gordon, now deceased at his father's hand, was a Frankston lout of the first order, a slaughter man by occupation, a big drinker and a big fighter and he had plenty of lout mates. Gordon died after a drinking binge with his dad Brian when, in a fit of rage, Brian raced off, grabbed a loaded 12 gauge shotgun and pointed it at Gordon. Gordon's last words were: "You haven't got the guts to pull the trigger." Wrong statement. Brian pulled the trigger and killed his son.

Looking after Gordon when he first started getting into trouble was really the beginning of my practice. The numerous cases I did for him were a big deal to me. I would go home and prep up each case and, being fairly green, I would not have any idea what I was doing. Ken Haines had appeared in the Court of Petty Sessions and the Magistrate's Court, and he would have been a good master. But he was too busy to sit down and take me through all the procedures in minute detail, so I muddled on as best I could. I was, after all, a solicitor acting as an advocate and not a barrister, as is usual in court. Sometimes ignorance is bliss. If I had been more aware of what was required, I probably would not have barged in the way I did.

There was one advantage to my inexperience. When you make a monumental blunder in court, it's a pretty lonely place as you're the only bloke in the whole place standing on your hind legs. You hope you don't make the same mistake again and the lesson is usually one that sticks in your mind for eternity. After all, only a mug doesn't learn from his mistakes; I'm living proof.

I can remember one occasion when a mate of Gordon's, by the name of Daryl Begg, was up on a charge of drunk and disorderly. Now there's no big deal about drunk and disorderly because invariably you get convicted and discharged – that is, no further penalty is imposed. However, on this occasion Daryl was outraged because he claimed he wasn't drunk and the coppers were staggered when I turned up and we were pleading not guilty. It caught them by surprise and well and truly off guard. To this day, I can remember with great fondness the bun fight that ensued in the old Frankston Magistrates' Court in defending a charge of drunk and disorderly. At the end of two days, Daryl was acquitted, much to the relief of everyone except the coppers. I was probably a bit too chirpy about the win, a tendency that has never been all that helpful to my relationship with the police.

Anyway, it was the start of bigger things for me as Daryl had other mates who got themselves into fairly regular bother and so the ball started to roll and the genesis of my criminal practice started to appear on the horizon. They were exciting times for me – times that I look back on with great nostalgia. I could not have begun to imagine then that doing those sorts of cases would ultimately take me around the world doing cases for the likes of Alan Bond et al.

I would sit in court every day that I possibly could and watch all the senior barristers with their grand reputations going through their paces. I personally accepted any case that came my way, which enabled me to appear in any court, whether I was defending a charge of speeding, drunk and disorderly, or (if I was really lucky) the occasional assault. I say "defend" because I never have and never will accept "Her Majesty's shilling" (prosecution cases). I have always preferred to appear for the "downtrodden and wrongly accused".

The thing I noticed was that the best criminal advocate in Melbourne at the time, Frank Galbally, was a solicitor and always appeared in his own matters, only occasionally briefing barristers.

I should explain. In the State of Victoria, when you are admitted to practise as a lawyer, you are admitted as a "Barrister and Solicitor of the Supreme Court". The differentiation in Victoria is that solicitors generally do not appear in court whereas barristers do. Some wankers (usually barristers) suggest that barristers are specialists and solicitors are general practitioners. There is nothing precluding solicitors from appearing, it's just that most don't. Uncle Frank had built his practice over many years on his own ability before judges and, especially, juries. When Galbally first started he gained a reputation for being prepared to tip out of bed at any hour of the day or night and go to any police station where a client may be held and give him advice. I soon learnt that advice of this nature was gold as far as detainees were concerned as it helped them not to feel isolated and abandoned in a police station. Galbally was someone I wanted to emulate and it was obvious to me that the only way to build a practice like his was to make myself the criminal law equivalent of an obstetrician – that is, to be available at all times for any person in any situation.

I gained a reputation for "tipping out" to the extent that I was called by the Australian Federal Police on Christmas Day two years in a row to advise people arrested at the airport in Melbourne on suspicion of attempting to smuggle drugs into Australia. Unfortunately, in those early years I was often lashed (not paid) by clients because I allowed my enthusiasm to outweigh my economic rationalism. In the long run it didn't really matter because I generated such a huge volume of work that I was soon briefing other barristers on a regular basis.

One of the most significant influences in my professional life was Philip Dunn, who is now a Queen's Counsel. On a good day Dunny is the best advocate I have ever seen. Dunny's most famous performance was in an armed robbery trial in which I had briefed him in the Supreme Court for a couple of old-fashioned stick-up merchants. The trial, many years ago now, was the first to be listed before the newly appointed Justice ("go home George") Hampel.

Dunny was in full flight for the entirety of the trial and the police ultimately mucked up, opening the escape door by the merest crack. The blunder by a witness from the Armed Robbery Squad was all Dunny needed and the trial came down to the final address to the jury. I had never seen anything like it before, nor have I since. Dunny rose to his feet to make his final address to the jury and in each hand was sock puppet! I couldn't believe my eyes. Dunny proceeded to conduct a mock (and mocking) discussion between the two puppets, who represented my two clients, Rocky Bob Starling and JR ("Not guilty") Ridgeway. Both of these blokes had been in plenty of strife over the years, particularly for stick-ups, and if they had been convicted on this trial they would have received double figures by way of sentence.

Justice Hampel's eyes nearly popped out of his head when Philip Dunn started his sock puppet routine, the purpose of which was to totally denigrate the Armed Robbery Squad, who had been caught out being rather economical with the truth and had now been made to pay, well and truly. The jury were riveted: I have never seen a jury pay such close attention to a final address in my life. There was not one person showing even the slightest sign of the fatigue that is pretty usual in those cases.

Chris Dane, QC, was appearing for Bob Starling and at the end of Phil Dunn's address he got up to make to his address and effectively said "How can you follow an address like that? All I've got to say is that my bloke's not guilty too!" With that Chris sat down.

The coppers had thought they had an overwhelming case and it was a mere formality that both Starling and Ridgeway would be convicted. So much so that Detective Sergeant David Newton who was then in the Armed Robbery Squad, and who – surprise, surprise – would be the Detective Superintendent in charge of the raid on my house some 20 years later, was so confident of success that I can recall him poking me in the chest outside the old Number 12 court in the Supreme Court and saying "If these blokes beat this, I'll give the fucking game away." He didn't have long to wait for his promised retirement because forty minutes later the jury came back and gave not guilty to the lot. You could have knocked the coppers over with a feather. They had just lost the unlosable trial! For their part, Rocky and JR stood up and, before they were even formally discharged by His Honour, walked over to the side of the dock, let themselves out and headed for the pub!

Getting back to Phil Dunn, I got to know Dunny very early in the piece when we were both young and enthusiastic. Even then he was a bloody good advocate and it was he who really encouraged me to become a solicitor advocate. I was talking to him one day and asked him why he wanted me to be a solicitor advocate, when I would only be doing work that would normally be briefed to him if I was a solicitor who did not do his own appearances. Phil's reply was that the more I conducted my practice the way I was – that is, making myself available twenty-four hours a day, seven days a week and running hard all the time – the more work I would generate. The more work I generated, the more I would brief Phil. Pretty good logic in retrospect. Over the years we had a very close professional relationship and I am and pleased and thankful to say that Dunny has stuck with me through all my trials and tribulations and, to this day, remains a mate.

Armed with Dunny's advice I continued to run hard over the years and from time to time clients would approach Phil direct. Because of the bar's ethics rules, he could not accept a direct brief from a client, so he would refer that client to me.

That is how I was instructed in my first murder case, in which Phil subsequently appeared for me. One day Phil rang and said "I have a couple of blokes I would like you to meet and they want to take you to the Flower Drum for lunch today if you're available." In those days the Flower Drum was not the internationally renowned five-star restaurant it is today; it was just a very, very good Chinese restaurant in Little Bourke Street at the bottom of a car park. The proprietor, Gilbert Lau, like myself, was running hard to build a business. I turned up for lunch at the Flower Drum and was introduced to two young blokes also on the way up in the world (their world, at least): Lewis Moran and his brother Desmond "Tuppence" (tuppence short of a pound) Moran. Lewis, who was to become my most important client over a thirty-year period, is now deceased, having been gunned down at the Council Club Hotel in Brunswick during the so-called gangland wars that afflicted Melbourne in the early 2000s. After the lunch Lewis asked if I was interested in acting for them if they found themselves in any bother in future. Could a rat eat a pound of cheese!

Of course I was, and so started a long relationship which only ended when Lewis was so senselessly gunned down after his release from jail.

By the time I was sent to jail in November 2001 Lewis had been charged with a drug trafficking offence, had been refused bail and had ended up in Port Phillip Prison with me. The powers that be at Port Phillip made it as difficult as they possibly could for Lewis and I to talk. However, we soon worked out that our respective units could attend the library at the same time each day, and that is what we did, chatting our way through library hour. Lewis was in jail with me when his son Jason was murdered by Victor Brincat, yet another former client of mine, at a football clinic in Essendon. Jason was killed in cold blood one Saturday morning attending the football clinic where his children played. The children were in the van with him when he was shot. An outrageous crime. Lewis had a stepson, Mark, who was also killed in the gangland wars. Unfortunately the only man left standing as I write is Tuppence.

When Jason was murdered the entire Victorian prison system happened to be locked down at the same time. The prisons were locked down because a gun had been found at Port Phillip Prison, where I was at the time. What a huge amount of excitement a shooter in jail caused! Every prisoner in the entire jail was locked in his cell for four days. I buzzed on the intercom system and spoke to control after I heard of Jason's murder on the ABC's midday news on the Saturday. I asked if I could speak to Lewis and was he alright? I was told to get fucked and without further ado I was hung up on. I immediately buzzed back again and said, "This is serious. I've just heard on the news that Lewis's son has been murdered, I would like to talk to him." Again I was told to get fucked, with the addition of: "If you buzz up one more time I will slot you [put you in the punishment solitary confinement cells for an unspecified period of time]". I did not get to see Lewis until the following Tuesday after we were let out.

It is interesting to note that, during that four-day lockdown, the Commissioner for Corrections, Kelvin Anderson, appeared on the ABC TV evening news and said there was nothing to worry about, each prisoner was being given his mandatory one hour a day out of his cell for the purpose of exercise.

In actual fact, that did not happen. We were locked down at about 1.30 pm on the Friday and were let out on the Tuesday about lunch time. During that period, we were not allowed to make a single phone call to our families, so they didn't know what had happened to us – whether we were well, hurt, sick or whatever. We were fed by the screws through the trap in the door. The screws were so lazy that they did not even bother to come and take our food scraps away for the entirety of the lockdown, so there were four days' worth of accumulated food scraps in our cells, together with dirty washing because we were not allowed out to do any washing. That is how you are treated in jail, while the powers that be are shown on television being, at best, careless with the truth.

When Lewis was finally to be released on bail I saw him

before he left. When he said goodbye, I said, "It's OK mate. I will see you when I finish my sentence." "No," he replied, "this is goodbye. I won't see you again." Lewis indicated to me that he knew he was going to be murdered and frankly, after Mark and Jason had been killed, he didn't really care whether he was killed or not.

Everybody refers to a "crime clan patriarch" when describing Lewis. In all the years I acted for him I defended one drink driving charge, which was dismissed, and two attempted murder charges. The first attempted murder charge arose over an argument about a car park outside the former Galleon night club in Russell Street, Melbourne. Lewis was a front-seat passenger in a car driven by "Nat the Rat". This case took place so long ago that the car, a brand-new Ford Fairlane, sported the first of the electric windows. The argument arose because there was a bloke standing in the empty car park and wouldn't move. It transpired that he was a bit of a knockabout himself and promptly told Nat to get fucked, whereupon he was shot – by whom is still a mystery.

Sitting in the front passenger seat of the car, Lewis had no idea that the pedestrian was going to be shot and to this day it is unclear as to where the gun was or who fired it. After the shooting Lewis and Nat the Rat bolted in double-quick time and were later arrested elsewhere in Melbourne. They were taken back to headquarters and given a thorough going over by the Major Crime Squad, as it was then. When I saw them on the Monday morning they were both black and blue. They had not been allowed to make a phone call for the entire weekend and said that, even if they had been able to call me, they wouldn't have bothered me because the coppers wouldn't have let them see me. When the trial finally arrived the Crown led no evidence because the shooter's identity was a problem and both accused were discharged.

The second attempted murder arose in strange circumstances. The victim rang his mother from a public phone out the front of the Earl of Lincoln hotel in Essendon and told her he had been shot in that hotel but didn't know by whom. He was taken to hospital and treated for a gunshot wound to the face. It was then that the police spoke to him and the story changed totally: he said he had been shot by Lewis Moran inside the Prince of Wales hotel in Mount Alexander Road, Moonee Ponds, some kilometres from the Earl of Lincoln.

To me, the whole case sounded trumped up from the start and when the matter came to a committal hearing (before trial) no firearm was presented as evidence. There was also no forensic evidence to show that this young man, who would have been bleeding profusely, had left any blood in the public phone outside the Prince of Wales. No blood was found in the Prince of Wales, there were no bullets or casings from any firearm found and there was no evidence that a firearm had been discharged. More importantly, the public bar at the Prince of Wales at the time was chock-a-block with drinkers and not one person came forward to say that they had seen or heard anything untoward. That case was discharged at committal and never went any further.

So to suggest that Lewis waged some sort of one-man war upon society is absurd. Yes, I concede that there now appears to be evidence that he became involved in the drug trade via his two sons Mark and Jason later in the piece, but for many years Lewis would not have a bar of drugs in any shape or form.

Clients can be important to you for two reasons. The first, and the obvious one for a criminal lawyer, is that the client constantly gets himself into strife and therefore regularly needs your services. The second, and this applied to Lewis Moran, is that the client, rather than get himself into a lot of trouble, knows people who get themselves into trouble and is prepared to recommend you to those people to act for them. This happened on a regular basis for the entire time during which I knew Lewis. I can't count how many clients he referred to me – but certainly there were hundreds – and I can trace just about all of my important clients or significant cases back to Lewis, even though they might be five or six times removed. Even the case of Alan Bond came to me indirectly through somebody who knew somebody who knew Lewis and had been referred to me by Lewis to act for them.

These referrals were just what the doctor ordered for a young criminal lawyer. They were blokes who got themselves into serious bother, not piddling little traffic offences. These blokes were committing armed robberies in the days when the targets were Armaguard vans or banks. They were the old-fashioned "stand and deliver" men, not the modern-day robber, invariably a junkie, who runs into a milk bar or a 7-eleven store armed with a dirty syringe to pinch a packet of smokes. These blokes were professionals and would quite openly state that that's what they did for a living.

As time went on, I was instructed to act for more and more of these characters and I was doing bail applications virtually on a daily basis. I was visiting prison regularly and in those days it was only Pentridge in Melbourne and you got to know all the screws. Things were done differently back then. Even the coppers behaved differently and, quite frankly, quite a few laughs were had among the police and the judges or magistrates and other barristers. These days everybody is terrified of political correctness and the humour seems to have very largely disappeared out of the court-room scene. Often even the crooks were in on the joke and you would hear a bit of a laugh from the back of the court where the dock was. The coppers played it a lot harder too but in a different manner. They expected to be grilled relentlessly in the witness box and didn't take it personally. On the other side of the coin it was also expected by the crooks and by the lawyers that the blokes would probably get a clip when they were arrested by the police. The standard reply when somebody turned up in the dock black and blue was that they had slipped on the steps coming into the city watch house while their hands were cuffed behind their backs. If I heard that explanation for a bloke's injuries once, I heard it a hundred times! We've got to remember that this all took place in the days before the term "political correctness" was even thought of. The police were robust, as were the crooks. As a young lawyer I soon learnt to be pretty resilient myself.

A classic example of this was the Moran boys, Mark and Jason. One night they were at the old Palace night club in St Kilda. The Palace was an interesting institution because not only did all the crooks hang out there but the coppers from the Major Crime Squad and Armed Robbery Squad drank there on the house with monotonous regularity. On any given night you could see, up one end, a bar full of coppers and, at the other end, a bar full of well-known "identities".

On the night in question, one of Mark and Jason's mates, one Ricky Kapaufs, had a rather large night and for a bit of a lark pulled a .357 pistol out of his suit pocket and promptly emptied it into the ceiling of the nightclub. You can imagine the effect that had on all the patrons in the nightclub. There were people ducking for cover right and left and, of course, with the coppers present, the action didn't take long to start. What could only be described as a huge blue ensued and at the end of that Kapaufs was arrested and charged with firearms offences. But a bigger issue was in relation to a copper called Peter Lalor and the allegation that Jason had gouged his eye out, or at least partially dislodged it, and needless to say the police were anxious to have young Jason "assist with their enquiries", as the euphemism goes.

Jason and Mark couldn't be found and because Lalor was

in the Major Crime Squad it was a big deal. To say that the police were actively pursuing Mark and Jason would be an understatement.

Things got a bit warm and I was contacted by Lewis to make an arrangement for the boys to surrender themselves for questioning. But there would be certain conditions attached to that – namely, that they would not be separated and I would be with them at all times. I rang Brian "the Skull" Murphy, who was an old-fashioned copper I had known for many years.

As an aside, Murphy, together with now Inspector Kim West, was probably the hardest copper I ever had to cross-examine. Murphy's tactic was always to try and start asking you questions. I would ask him the question "Sergeant, now, on the night in question…" and he would come back with "Was that a Tuesday or a Wednesday?" "I would say that doesn't really matter." "No, I need to know, so I can get my thoughts in order, Mr Fraser, to answer your questions properly." In the old days there was a term for this: it was called using a "brick". That meant that the witness would build a brick wall around you, metaphorically speaking, if you didn't ask the questions correctly or answer their questions correctly, and Murphy was a classic; he had a brick in every pocket! Kim West was in a different category altogether. Formerly the world's fattest copper, in the old days he was renowned in the northern suburbs for waging war on all the louts. They were both old-fashioned coppers and knew every trick in the book.

I spoke to Murphy and made an arrangement to present Mark and Jason one evening at their offices. It was agreed that they would not be separated and I would be present at both of their interviews.

At the designated time I arrived at the Major Crime Squad offices to be met not by Murphy but rather by Detective Sergeant Peter Spence. In the old days Spence and I locked horns on many, many occasions and we certainly enjoyed a robust relationship. "No Murphy and therefore no deal," was Spence's greeting. I said, "Well hang on a minute, we're leaving." He said, "I don't think so."

Jason was immediately grabbed and thrown into one interview room and the door slammed and locked. Mark was thrown into another, that door also being slammed and locked. I started to have a bit to say about going back on their agreement, whereupon Spence picked me up (he is a very large man) and physically threw me out of the Major Crime Squad offices. I was furious at this behaviour but they wouldn't let me back in to see my clients again. I was told to fuck off. I said, "We'll see about that, I'm going to make a formal compliant."

I went to the ground floor of the St Kilda Road Police Headquarters, where this was all taking place, and asked to see the duty inspector because I wanted to make a formal complaint about the behaviour of the Major Crime Squad.

I waited and waited and waited – waited a couple of hours, in fact – until the duty inspector turned up. He looked at me and I looked at him. He said, "You want to make a complaint?" I said, "Yes, I've been thrown out of the Major Crime Squad and they told me to fuck off." He replied, "Well, I'm telling you as well: fuck off." I said, "You can't do that. You've got to take the complaint from me." He said, "No, I don't", and that was the end of that.

In the meantime, while I was downstairs left sitting like a shag on a rock, the coppers had interviewed Jason and Mark, who of course had nothing to say and refused to answer any questions. They were both charged and whisked out the back door of St Kilda Road and taken to the City Watch House, where a bail justice was brought in. They were charged with serious offences and bail was refused.

By the time I got wind of this, bail had already been refused and the coppers thought it was a huge joke that I was too late. Not to be deterred, I raced straight in to the City Watch House, looked at the register of prisoners in order to see the name of the bail justice who had refused bail. I then drove up to Carlton, picked up the bail justice from his hotel where he was a publican, drove him back to the City Watch House and made a bail application on the basis that my clients had not been represented when their bail was originally refused. Bail was promptly granted.

He who laughs last laughs longest and I thought it was huge joke because, by the time I got back with the bail justice to make the bail application, all the coppers had departed, congratulating themselves on having locked up Jason and

Mark Moran. The coppers were furious when they heard that I had outsmarted them.

These sorts of stories could go on and on. Often, to both sides of the fence – police and crooks – the whole thing was a game. The crooks tried not to get caught and the coppers tried to catch. If either side took the odd shortcut in order to achieve their desired result well, that's the way the game was played. Most blokes copped it on the chin, in many cases quite literally.

One bloke who was referred to me by Lewis Moran was called Tommy the Fibber – because he was rather careless with the truth. On this particular night, I was called in to Russell Street Police Headquarters to the Armed Robbery Squad offices. There was a long straight hall, with one bench seat and linoleum on the floor. As I walked around the corner, I saw a bloke, which turned out to be Tommy, sitting with his legs astride, his elbows rested on his knees and a huge pool of blood at his feet. As I approached, he looked up. His face was black and blue, one eye was closed and he could hardly talk because of a split lip. I was a bit surprised to see Tommy in this state because he had a reputation for being able to look after himself. "In God's name what has happened to you?" I asked. Tommy looked up and grinned and said, "Let's call it a dead heat." I said, "What do you mean, a dead heat?" He replied:

Well, I was asleep in bed, I heard this banging at the front door. I immediately grabbed the pistol I had under my pillow, raced down the hallway and I was about to let a couple off through the door when I realised, hang on this might be the coppers so I raced back, hid the gun and stood behind the door. As soon as the door was smashed in, as it invariably was, I just let go. I decked the first three in the door, knocked them straight out, but then the other ten or so that came in afterwards kicked the living Jesus out of me. On that basis I'm happy to call it a dead heat.

There was never any complaint made about Tommy's treatment by the police. He signed the interview register stating that he was satisfied with his treatment by the police. That's the way it was in those days. He was man enough to say, well, I got the first three in the door, I'll cop what comes after that. Just imagine the hue and cry these days if an incident like that took place. There would be questions in parliament, followed by all sorts of mealy-mouthed recriminations.

While on that topic, it's worth noting that Melbourne's Armed Robbery Squad, which was recently disbanded, had a fearsome reputation among crooks as being pretty violent coppers. The squad's reply to that was always: "We deal with violent men, therefore we need to be violent too." Believe it or not, I accept that reasoning to some degree but when you see the video tape that recently took place of a bloke being belted by a large number of Armed Robbery Squad coppers in an interview room, that is not good enough. If you are dealing with an old-fashioned armed robber – that is, one of the true hard men of this town – then he expects to be dealt with in a harsh fashion as well and he usually gets what he was expecting. But to prey on weaker, defenceless blokes is not on.

Lewis and Tuppence came from a background where it was almost to be expected that they, too, would end up leading a life of crime. Their mother, Belle Moran, had been a nurse for one Charlie Wyatt, who was an abortionist back in the days when abortion was illegal and you could go to jail for committing it. In the late 1960s, William Kaye, QC, (later Justice Kaye of the Supreme Court) conducted an inquiry into abortion in Melbourne and Belle and Charlie featured prominently in that enquiry.

Lewis's dad, Des Senior, was the SP (Starting Price) bookmaker at the Newmarket Hotel for a good many years. SP bookmaking is illegal in Victoria. Lewis started off his career as a pickpocket and later moved into SP bookmaking himself, with a little bit of debt collecting on the side.

I have a view of SP bookmaking that is fairly benevolent. I think, in fact, that it often provides a service but these days, with the growth of the betting and gambling industries and the huge Government rake-offs that follow, SP bookmaking is on the nose and is frowned upon. The penalties imposed for SP bookmaking are absurdly high but it created a lot of work for me when the government of the day, in an attempt to appease the powers that be in the Victorian Totalisator Agency Board (TAB), tried to stamp out SP bookmaking by creating Police Task Force Zebra, whose specific job was to track down and eliminate the SPs. The fun and games that followed lasted a couple of years and while SP bookmaking was largely stamped out, it is now making a comeback. The question is: so what? The amount that a small SP bookmaker in a pub holds will make absolutely no difference to a TAB or to the government's rake-off.

When Task Force Zebra was at its height, there were a couple of teams of coppers running around Melbourne with twelve pound sledge hammers smashing in doors and trying like hell to grab blokes while they were conducting an SP operation. The ingenuity of the SP operators became well known. Tricks such as sitting on a toilet with the lid up and your legs apart with a card table in front of you... the minute the coppers raced in the door, everything was swept down the toilet and flushed away. It then got to the stage where the coppers woke up to what was going on; I even did a case where, before racing in the door, the police disconnected the sewerage outlet pipe and had one man stand there with a bucket. As the coppers ran in the door and the toilet was flushed, all the SP bookmaking slips were flushed out into the bucket. Mission accomplished, SP bookmaker pinched and a huge fine imposed. These were pretty rough-and-tumble days and, for me as a young criminal lawyer, very stimulating and a lot of fun.

Not everything that crossed my desk at that time entailed someone's neck being on the line. One of the cases generated by Haines Blakie and Polites's general practice was a standing brief as honorary lawyers to the then Victorian Football League Umpires Association. The VFLUA had been in existence for a while, with not much call for our services, but what there was, I jumped at handling for the umpires.

Life was different then, without the emphasis on money and conditions that now exists, and there was a far more laid-back attitude to footy generally. It was still a game then and I miss those days. Things started to change when Alan Aylett became president and Jack Hamilton secretary in about the late 1970s. The age of footy as a business was dawning.

One Thursday night at the start of the 1981 season, Hamilton, who as both player and administrator was not renowned for his subtlety, showed up at a training night for the umpires and presented them with new contracts. The contracts were to be signed by the end of training or everyone would be sacked. So much for conciliation. Needless to say, the umpires were not happy with this state of affairs and an emergency meeting was called for that same night at The Royal Oak pub in Richmond. As honorary solicitor I was asked to attend.

The late Harry Beitzel was in charge of the umpires and was all in favour of signing the new contracts without further ado. The umpires were furious at the League's attitude and after a highly charged meeting a motion was passed unanimously that all the senior umpires would resign en masse as a message of solidarity.

I clearly recall being in the public phone at the front of

the pub (no mobiles in those days) ringing "H" (as Beitzel was known) and conveying the happy news that he no longer had a list of senior umpires. H could not believe his ears and kept raving on that the umpires could not strike. Wrong, H. We are not striking: this is a mass resignation and you have no umpires for Saturday.

I was nominated as spokesperson for the umpires and so began my first case over which I was catapulted into the media glare. Very exciting for a young lawyer when you take into account the quasi-religious fervour that surrounds footy in Victoria and the mass media coverage that it attracts.

Friday morning brought a meeting of the League at its headquarters, which the umpires and I were asked to attend. I advised the umps that, if anyone started to give us a spray rather than negotiate in a sensible manner, we would walk out as a group.

The meeting started – and so did a couple of the board members, giving us an almighty serve about how we were ruining football, etc., etc. In accordance with our agreement and much to the astonishment of the League, we then walked out of the meeting and headed back to my office to await developments. We did not have to wait long before Aylett was on the phone trying to square off and reconvene the meeting. We agreed to meet again later in the day.

This time the meeting was more cordial but the League would not negotiate further on the contracts while we were technically, due to our resignations, not employed by it.

A stalemate followed and much to everyone's surprise the umpires did not cave in. Come Friday afternoon, the league had no senior umpires for the weekend fixtures.

Saturday came and a whole group of junior umpires were promoted for their one and only senior fixture. The umpires met at the VFLUA president's home in Essendon and some went to the footy to watch a game. The rest of us continued to meet and fend off the media, who by now were camped outside the president's house.

Early the next week the League caved in and, in a comprehensive win for our side, all of the umpires' demands were agreed to at a meeting of the League. We were invited to drinks after the meeting in the board room in an effort to repair the relationship. The get-together was rather frosty but the umpires had won a great victory. I was made an honorary life member of the VFLUA and at the annual dinner dance at season's end I was presented with a wonderful oil painting. The life membership certificate and the painting are hanging in my house as I write this book.

The umpires stuck together like glue, with not one man even looking like he was getting the wobbles. This unity enabled them to win a comprehensive victory that the media had generally considered was unwinnable against such formidable opposition.

The more experienced I became, the harder and more serious were the cases I defended. The daily bout of shoplifting, speeding, assault and burglary cases gradually started to give way to armed robberies. More importantly, what changed the entire scene in criminal law everywhere was the advent of the drug industry.

When drugs first started to appear it was usually cannabis and a little LSD. The real no-hopers were into the heroin (or "smack" or "hammer and tack", as it is referred to colloquially) and most of the cannabis was in the form of Buddha sticks, which were brought in from Bali very cheaply and distributed. Buddha sticks were cannabis wound around a stick.

The drug scene started to get nasty when the Romanians became involved in the heroin trade. Any drug is highly profitable for the trafficker, from the importer all the way down to the street-level distributor. In very broad terms what happens is that drugs are imported or manufactured in as pure a form as possible. Take the example of the methyl amphetamine, or "speed", that is usually "cooked" (manufactured) in this country. The cook manufactures it pure – which, if he is really good at his job, is somewhere in the vicinity of 75 to 80 per cent pure. But the cook never, ever sells pure, so what arrives "pure" from the cook has already been cut in half – that is, diluted by 50 per cent by the manufacturer, with one kilogram becoming two. Drugs are diluted all the way down the supply chain, until, in the most extreme instances (usually methyl amphetamine), they hit the street (usually nightclubs) at two to five per cent purity, the rest being glucose or some other cutting agent.

A new drug, crystalline methamphetamine (crystal meth, or "ice"), which is methyl amphetamine but in a pure form, is sold in crystals looking something like salt crystals. A piece of crystal meth the size of a match head can keep you going for a couple of days. It is cheap, easy to manufacture and readily available. This is a frightening prospect as I have seen numerous kids (young twenty-somethings) in jail who have literally cooked their brains with the use of this drug. I have been told that the euphoria from the ingestion of crystal meth is extraordinary and that you go and go and go. Sometimes these kids have not slept for a couple of weeks. Sleep, of course, is the body's way of regenerating itself or renewing itself and you can imagine the damage that it does to mind and body when you stay awake for that period of time. These kids are now mentally ill and are not in a position to ever take a meaningful place in our society again. It is a truly shocking problem and one that governments have got to come to terms with.

Is drug use a health issue or is it a law enforcement issue? The fact that I took cocaine (a drug of natural origin) does not mean I am sticking up for it but from my observations, the drugs that are the most damaging to anyone's physique seem to be the chemically based drugs – LSD, methyl amphetamine, crystal meth and ecstasy among them. The drugs that you seem to be able to come back from are the naturally occurring substances – heroin, cannabis and cocaine. I think your body is able to metabolise those drugs and thus, if you abstain for a period of time, you'll eliminate them from your system and have some hope of functioning adequately again.

From my observation of the heroin trade, it's not the heroin that kills you but the lifestyle that goes with it. I acted on one occasion, many years ago, for a theatre nurse at the Alfred Hospital who had been a heroin addict for many years. Regardless of his addiction, he had been able to continue to conduct an outwardly normal life, including being in theatre in the usual manner. He had a strict regime as to how much heroin he would take and would make sure he ate and kept himself as fit as he could. His routine was to get up in the morning and not have his morning hit until he had showered, shaved and had breakfast. Then he would have a hit, which got him through to lunchtime. He would have another hit with his lunch which, in turn, saw him through to the end of the day. He then went home and crashed out after having one last hit for the day. I know this sounds extraordinary but it is the truth. If you observe somebody on speed, by contrast, they are ratty and irrational, with scattered thought processes and a complete inability to sit still.

Which reminds me of the Moran boys, Jason and Mark. They were little boys when I first met them and Mark was nicknamed Handsome Harry because he was tall, athletic, well built and good looking. Jason was a good kid as well, always very polite to me right to the end, but it was interesting to note that as Jason got older, his behaviour got more erratic, particularly when he drank and took drugs. Once the drugs and the drink were on board, Jason had an unpredictable streak that made him likely to do anything. The erratic behaviour caused Detective Sergeant Peter Spence of the Major Crime Squad to observe to me one day that Jason will end up either dead or killing someone. Sure enough, that is what happened, only in the reverse order.

One person who was referred to me by another knockabout, Michael Pagonis, also a friend of Lewis Moran, was a bloke called Big Tony Weatherald. (I don't know why so many crooks are nicknamed "big". Maybe the size aspect is somehow awe inspiring.) Big Tony was a con man by occupation. Con men are the most fun to act for: they are invariably "hail fellow well met", very personable, believable and likable. The only trouble is, they do all that with other people's money. Big Tony had a few problems over the years with helping himself to other people's money, but on one particular occasion he had got himself in well and truly over his eyebrows. If he had been convicted of the offence he was charged with – namely fraud in relation to some opals – he would have gone to jail.

I don't know where these people bob up from and it has never ceased to amaze me how many different types of people exist in our society that we don't even know about. But Big Tony had stumbled on a doctor, Ted Wellstead. Ted had been a doctor in the army and had been charged with manslaughter following the death of a patient on the operating table. He was acquitted but thereafter hated the coppers, not that he made this public knowledge. Somehow Big Tony had met Doctor Ted and found out about his resentment. This was very handy because Big Tony desperately needed an adjournment of his fraud case so that the matter would hopefully cool off and he may not go to jail.

Doctor Ted immediately placed Big Tony in hospital. He contacted me and advised that he had started treating Tony and that he was suffering from some rare disease whereby he had extreme sensitivity of the skin and any movement was excruciating. This went on and on for months – Tony in and out of hospital, case unable to proceed. Each time, Doctor Ted, who looked absolutely impeccable as far as his credentials were concerned, came along to court and gave evidence. Ultimately, the police surgeon went to visit Big Tony in hospital to diagnose him for himself. Ted had prompted Tony as to what to do. Tony was sitting in bed with a frame over him so that the blankets were not touching his skin. When the police surgeon came in and pulled the blankets back, Tony screamed and nearly went through the roof. The police surgeon attended court and gave evidence that Big Tony was too sick to attend. Problem solved. The matter ended up going away because in the interim the alleged victim of the fraud had died.

Big Tony particularly liked opals but he met his match on one occasion with Ross Christianos, an opal dealer from South Australia with a bit of form. Christianos has mines at Andamooka and at Cooper Pedy. Another thing Christianos had was some very low quality Chilean opals which he could not unload. Until I saw these stones I didn't even know that Chile produced opals. It does, but they are of a much inferior quality to the Australian opal. Christianos had worked out, however, that if you boiled these opals in glycerine they took on the appearance of Australia's best quality black opal, with red highlights – the most expensive type and highly sought after overseas.

Big Tony was trying to get some opals on credit from Christianos, which he subsequently did. The only trouble was that the opals were the boiled Chilean opal and not Cooper Pedy black opal. When Tony tried to do his deal, the pur-chaser had the opals tested and the whole deal came unstuck because they were exposed for what they really were.

Christianos wanted his money. Tony wouldn't pay. (Tony probably never intended paying.) Things went from bad to worse, with Christianos threatening all sorts of dire conse-quences if he was not paid. I eventually became involved, acting for Tony, and I arranged to travel to Adelaide with him to discuss the matter with Christianos. Big Tony arranged for a mate of his, Tom Eriksen, a "private detective" at the time, who always carried a fire arm, to travel with us to Adelaide as "muscle" in case Christianos played up. Tom also brought an offsider. I will never forget the look on the faces of the airline staff when Big Tony hauled his shooter out and slammed it on the counter. Tom and his sidekick did the same. I couldn't believe these blokes were armed and how cool everybody was about it. In those days it was a lot easier to get a firearms licence than it is today.

We travelled from the airport to the Adelaide foothills to see Christianos at his house where we all went into a big conference room. Erikson's offsider sat at one end of the table and Christianos at the other. It was the only time I've ever been in a room where everybody (except me) was armed. Christianos sat forward and I said to him, "Hang on, you've got a gun on." He started to splutter and Eriksen unholstered his gun and put it on the table, saying "Put yours on the table too, otherwise we are all out of here." That relieved my tension a little. Until we left, and I was told why Eriksen's offsider was sitting at the other end of the table. For the entire meeting he had been sitting there with his gun under the table pointed straight at Christianos's legs. Once again a commercial settlement had been arranged and Big Tony lived to fight another day.

But Big Tony really hit the big time when he met a senior person in the Krug Thai bank. Tony had been provided with promissory notes which could be used as secondary collateral for loans. These notes were each worth millions of US dollars and the allegation was that Big Tony then went around the world negotiating some of these promissory notes for extraordinary sums of money. One French bank was relieved of US$40 million and when its management were spoken to they denied that it had ever happened. Banks can be a bit sensitive about admitting they have been defrauded.

Chapter 3
Bigger and Better Things

*Men stumble over the truth from time to time, but
most pick themselves up and hurry off as if nothing
had happened!*
WINSTON CHURCHILL

Big Tony Weatherald might have been trotting around the
world securing major deals and doing very nicely for himself,
but he made one fatal mistake. He negotiated the smallest of
his promissory notes (US$1 million) with a pearl dealer in
Broome. The pearl dealer found out the notes were in fact
forgeries and all hell broke lose. Big Tony was flying back
into Australia when he was arrested at Melbourne Airport
with about US $20 million worth of promissory notes in his
briefcase. He was taken by the Australian Federal Police and
charged. It was a Friday afternoon, as I recall, when I attended
the Old Melbourne Magistrates' Court for the purpose of
conducting a bail application for Big Tony. The application

was successful and he was released on bail.

This case opened a can of worms of monumental proportions. Money and promissory notes were flying all around the world and when I briefed Phil Dunn to appear in this matter with me it was the start of an extraordinary ride.

Tony's defence was, at all times, that the Krung Thai Bank not only knew about his use of these notes but condoned it and, further, that there was a senior person in the bank who was aware of and a party to the scheme.

When Big Tony was arrested, allegations were immediately made that he had negotiated these notes all over the world and that vast quantities of money had been obtained and had somehow disappeared. Back in Australia Big Tony always said he was bereft of cash and no one could demonstrate that he had vast quantities of wealth hanging around anywhere.

Our first instruction was to travel to Monte Carlo, London and Geneva to discuss the negotiating of these notes with the lawyers and financiers who had carried out the transactions on Big Tony's behalf. Phil Dunn and I initially travelled to London, where we met with lawyers, then on to Monte Carlo, where we went to Beau Soleil, which is the French town immediately up the hill behind Monte Carlo. There we discussed these matters for a couple of days with a former Australian lawyer who subsequently ended up in trouble in relation to other unrelated money laundering activities. Phil and I decided to drive from Monte Carlo to Geneva and we enjoyed a delightful day travelling via the Mont Blanc tunnel. We discussed matters in Geneva and the interesting aspect was that everybody who was supposedly a victim of Big Tony denied that any money had been lost at any time. It became pretty obvious that the institutions involved, including a Swiss bank and a large French bank, would rather write off any losses (no matter how big) than have publicity that would show they were vulnerable to fraud. Of course, if there were no other victims apart from the one Australian pearl trader who had made the initial complaint, this could only help our case.

We returned to Australia and advised Big Tony of all of this. Things were starting to look good until the brief of evidence arrived. This document contained numerous statements from employees quite high up in the Krung Thai Bank saying that: one, the wording of the notes was different from the official Krung Thai Bank notes; and, secondly, the official bank seal was different from that used by the bank. For Dunny and me, though, the notes bore a striking similarity to the real thing, albeit with some minor variations. The seal was virtually the same as the bank seal, but again with slight variations. We didn't do anything further about that at that time but the bank employees' statements all pointed in one direction: that the notes were forgeries.

An allegation was then made that Big Tony had been involved in another fraud on a substantial European bank that had a North American office in Dallas, Texas. Our instructions were then to travel to the United States to interview the head of this bank (which I can't name because it too denied ever having been defrauded). Arriving in Dallas was like stepping into a completely different world. The head of the bank presented as the quintessential Texan: large, loud, wearing a suit with cowboy boots and a ten gallon hat. Talk about a stereotype! Keeping this bloke on the topic of the alleged fraud against the bank was virtually impossible. He started going on about the car-jackings being committed by coloured people or Hispanics in Dallas, saying he would fix any of them at any time, should they endeavour to car-jack him. At this point he pulled up one leg of his trousers and produced a hand gun from his cowboy boots. We couldn't believe our eyes. I said, "Calm down for Christ's sake! We are having a conference in a hotel about an alleged fraud on your bank and I'm here on behalf of the person who is alleged to have carried out the fraud with your compliance. Nothing to do with car-jacking, so put the bloody gun away." He did that and when the conference concluded he invited us out for lunch.

We were to be driven to lunch by the manager's driver and as I got into the car I noticed, believe it or not, another hand gun in a clip next to the driver's seat. He opened the glove box to show me yet another hand gun. I couldn't believe it! The restaurant was in an area rather like Melbourne's Lygon Street (a little Italy) except that there was not a person to be seen, even though it was lunchtime on a Friday. As we approached the restaurant, the driver, who had a head set on, radioed through, stating our estimated distance away. On arrival we were asked to sit in the car while two security men walked from the restaurant, opened the door and escorted us in. We couldn't believe the fact that supposedly the greatest democracy on earth was so unsafe that you couldn't walk from your car to the restaurant unguarded. Maybe the banker actually had something to go on when he said the place was unsafe. We came back to Australia with the information given to us by this bloke: that there had been no fraud on his bank.

There was a very strong smell of conspiracy to this whole case but we were bound by our instructions. The committal proceedings were held in Adelaide and person after person from the Krung Thai bank came forward to say that nobody had permission to negotiate these notes and that the notes were forgeries and further that the bank had lost tens of millions of dollars as a result of this illegal behaviour.

Dunny and I smelt far too many rats in this. The crunch came when we were looking at the documents and realised that the paper stock seemed the same as the official bank stock; the typesetting and printing on the documents were the same, even though the wording was slightly different; and the bank seal was the same, even though again the words were slightly different. We sent off the paper, the ink, the seal and the seal ink for analysis. And guess what? It all came back as being the same paper, same printing, same ink and same seal as those the bank used. In other words, it was clear that somebody inside the bank must be in on the rort – if in fact it was a rort, which Big Tony, of course, specifically denied.

When the committal was held we didn't run anything to do with the nature of the documentation, save to say that we cross-examined every person from the Dallas bank and received confirmation that they knew nothing about this. After Big Tony was committed for trial, we then took this matter up with the prosecuting powers and laid out before them what we knew about the "same paper" argument. We pointed out that it was most likely someone in the bank who was a co-conspirator in this and that, as a result, there had been no fraud on the bank and this case could only proceed if the bank produced evidence that they knew nothing about it consequently all charges against Big Tony were withdrawn. The prosecution had fallen apart.

The allegation had been that over one and a half billion dollars worth of promissory notes had been negotiated around the world. Whether Big Tony had been involved in all of them, nobody really knew but it was a very large case and would have resulted in a huge penalty if he had been convicted. But we made the whole thing go away and Tony was extremely grateful. He would always say to us that one day he would repay us in full for what we had done for him.

About a year or so later, Tony rang me and said he was about to repay his debt to us in full, with a bit more on top for good measure, and that Phil Dunn and I were to meet him at The Latin restaurant in Melbourne for lunch the next day. He wouldn't say any more about it, other than that we should be at The Latin at 1 pm. We were full of intrigue the next day as we walked into The Latin, only to see, sitting at the table with Tony, none other than Alan Bond. It turns out that Bondy was a mate of Big Tony's and, as most readers of this book would know, Alan Bond had just got himself into a substantial amount of trouble over ownership of the French impressionist painting La Promenade by Edouard Manet.

Sadly, Big Tony was to suffer a heart attack one morning a few months later while taking his constitutional in the local park. Big Tony had played league football in three states and was very well known, so his funeral was enormous. I attended with my then partners Brian Rolfe and Bob Galbally. If ever there was an example of why you should never engage the services of a priest who did not know the deceased, then this funeral was it. The sky pilot looked around the crowded church and made the observation: "Isn't it wonderful to see the church full today and know that Tony touched everyone here." There was silence for a few seconds and then the place erupted with laughter because Tony had a habit of "touching" all his mates at one time or another – only not in the sense the priest intended!

At that stage Bondy's former company, Bell Resources, had crashed and was being wound up. Bell Resources was a failure to the tune of A$1.2 billion and the journalist Trevor

Sykes, then from the *Australian Financial Review*, had been agitating non-stop since its crash for Bondy to be charged with a cash strip of the company. Trevor Sykes's allegation was that Bond Corporation had bought its way into Bell Resources purely for the cash on hand. At the time of the takeover Bell had hundreds of millions of dollars in the bank and held BHP shares to the tune of hundreds of millions of dollars as well. Once Bond Corporation took over Bell, all of the BHP shares were sold and converted to cash, which was then transferred to Bond Corporation in an endeavour to stave off its impending collapse. The cash in the bank was all transferred too, hence the term cash strip.

Having joined Bondy for lunch at The Latin that day, by four o'clock that afternoon I had instructions to act as his solicitor in relation to all of his outstanding or potential criminal matters. This was the biggest case going in the country at the time and I was ecstatic at receiving those instructions. I can remember stepping into Lonsdale Street, ringing my office and telling them I didn't care what I had on the next day, it was all to be cancelled. I had just pulled Alan Bond as a client and I would be in Perth the next morning to receive his instructions.

Bondy and I spent the entire next day with his Perth solicitors, who gave me a frosty reception to say the least. The solicitors were a firm called Parker and Parker and they were absolutely furious that I had received instructions to act for Bondy in the criminal matters. Bondy kept trying to reassure them with the fact that they would continue to act for him in all commercial matters, just not the criminal matters.

By about eight o'clock that night, after being left twiddling my thumbs and staring at the wall in a small conference room (and I mean small: maybe three by three metres) for an entire day without being offered so much as a cup of tea, I returned to Melbourne with Bondy's full authority and an undertaking by Parker and Parker to co-operate with me in every way possible while I was acting for Bond in relation to the criminal matters.

At this time, Trevor Sykes was not the only one agitating; there was also a journalist by the name of Paul Barry, who was then giving (and continues to give) Bondy plenty of grief – and to say that Paul and I have had a frank exchange of views would understate the matter. When I was charged and my committal proceedings were on, who should turn up to cover my committal for *The Bulletin* but Paul Barry.

Readers may recall Barry's book, *The Rise and Fall of Alan Bond*, in which he is rather less than complimentary about Bondy and suggests in no uncertain terms that there are still vast quantities of money hidden around the world that the shareholders of Bell Resources and Bondy's original company, Bond Corporation, have all missed out on. Barry, I recall, travelled to Switzerland to try to talk with Gorg Bolag, who was alleged to have been Bondy's money man in Switzerland, all to no avail.

When I started receiving documentation in relation to

Bond it was obvious that all of these matters concerning him were huge and complex. In relation to La Promenade, the allegations were that Bond had purchased the painting through Bond Corporation and had thereafter improperly transferred the painting, which was worth some millions of dollars, to Dallhold, which was Bonds' private company, in which he personally owned 99.9% of the shares. The transfer of the painting from Bond Corporation to Dallhold was allegedly to the detriment of the Bond Corporation shareholders as really Dallhold had received the painting for nothing, thereby defrauding the Bond Corporation shareholders of the value of that painting.

Bondy had Lady Angela Neville (a cousin of Queen Elizabeth II) acting for him as his art advisor and purchaser and we had to speak to Lady Angela as well as to other lawyers and accountants about the financial setups of Bond Corporation and Dallhold.

It later also became apparent that we would be best to speak to all of these people about Bell Resources and where the money had gone because Trevor Sykes and Paul Barry's agitations were not diminishing and it was starting to look like Bondy was also going to be charged with the Bell Resources cash strip.

Bondy instructed me that I would need to travel to London, to the Channel Islands (Jersey in particular) and to Zurich and Zug in Switzerland. Zug is the oldest and smallest of the cantons (states) in the Swiss confederation. It also has the most liberal tax laws and is the wealthiest. The good residents of Zug have for hundreds of years made their living out of looking after other peoples' money and as a result have developed a very strong disinclination to be of assistance to other people who are overly nosey about what they are doing with their clients' money. These were certainly exciting times travelling all over the world for Bondy discussing such matters with so many heavy hitters.

While we were still preparing our defence for La Promenade, Trevor Sykes and Paul Barry finally got their way and Bond was charged over the Bell Resources cash strip. At the time, this was the biggest corporate fraud in Australia's history. For that reason and because Bondy had headed the syndicate that won the America's Cup yachting trophy for the first time from the Americans, the case generated huge publicity not only in Australia but all around the world.

One of the most interesting aspects of the run around the world chasing the money allegedly belonging to Bell Resources shareholders was the amount of time I spent in Zug. Zug, being so old, also had its own criminal code and that code contained the most extraordinary privilege that I have ever seen. It effectively stated that "if to answer a question would tend to diminish a person's standing in the community then that person was not required to answer that question" – a get-out-of-jail-free card if ever there was one! This privilege was to ultimately put an end to any enquiry that our Australian authorities were making as to the whereabouts of any Bond or Bell Resources money in Switzerland – just as, after some years and a number of false starts, the Australian Federal Police thought they had finally got their act together and would get Gorg Bolag into the witness box in Zug with a view to ascertaining whether he currently held, or had previously held, any money on the behalf of Bond.

When we arrived in Switzerland for about the fourth shot at getting Bolag into the box, all reasons for adjournments had been exhausted. The case was going on, come hell or high water. I was instructed by Bond to act for Bolag and travelled to Switzerland for that purpose. I briefed a local lawyer who was an advocate and had experience in this area. The two of us appeared for Bolag before the Attorney General for the Canton of Zug and, despite our protests, Bolag found himself in the witness box.

The proceedings made it to the end of the first morning. Bolag had wrongly thought he was smarter than the officials examining him and made a complete botch of the matter. He had thought it would be smart to answer questions rather than rely on the privilege that was available to him under the old Zug cantonal criminal code. I clearly remember how, when lunchtime on that first day came, Bolag left the witness box and the other lawyers to go for lunch. He was very chuffed with how he was going and I was livid with his performance. I recall standing outside the Attorney General's office and being asked by Bolag "How do you think

I went?" I said to all of the other lawyers, "You go and have some lunch on your own. I'm talking to Bolag." I dragged him off and read him the riot act over lunch. He was quite chastened because he genuinely thought he had gone well in his performance before the court that morning when in fact, if he had kept on going, he could have landed himself in jail for perjury.

I wrote out in long hand the privilege that was available to him and I firmly instructed him that this was all he was to say to every question from here on in.

A chastened Gorg Bolag returned to the witness box after lunch and, much to my relief, followed my instructions. Every question asked of him thereafter was met with a reading of the privilege. The Commonwealth of Australia and the Swiss authorities were most unhappy at this change of events. However, they persisted with asking questions and at the end of two days the Attorney General asked Bolag whether he was going to answer every question by relying on the privilege available to him. Bolag answered in the affirmative. The Attorney General then concluded the proceedings, saying there was nothing to be gained and that he could not and would not force Bolag to answer questions that would be in breach of the privilege available to him.

As a result of Gorg sticking to his guns, the entire Commonwealth case against Bond and Bolag for secreting any monies into Switzerland or against Bolag for having dealt improperly with any of Bond's money fell in a hole and those proceedings have never been resurrected, nor are they likely to be.

Meanwhile the first committal proceedings against Bond for the transferral of La Promenade had proceeded and it was during those proceedings that Bondy's famous "I can't remember" defence was run. It was clear that Bond's memory was not good and it became apparent that he had been receiving some medical treatment from a psychiatrist in Sydney in relation to his inability to recall everything that had happened during his heyday as head of Bond Corporation and Bell Resources. What followed caused a lot of angst to the prosecution and involved us in a lot of work.

In short, Bond said that he could not recall details of what had happened in a lot of the transactions or the board meetings where decisions had been made either in relation to the transfer of the La Promenade painting or relating to the Bell Resources cash strip.

We spoke to the psychiatrist in Sydney, who was under the impression that Bondy was suffering from a degenerative disease of the brain. We spent an enormous amount of time having Bond's brain scanned and getting experts to look at those scans. It became apparent that there were areas of degeneration in Bondy's brain and that these could well affect his memory. It was never suggested that the deterioration in his brain had affected his ability to make decisions at the time; rather, that now he was unable to clearly remember and therefore could not give us adequate instructions as to his defence. If this was extended to its logical conclusion, then he could not properly defend himself and therefore all the charges should be withdrawn on the basis of his medical condition. This suggestion brought a tirade of ridicule from the press and we called expert after expert at the committal to attest that Bond was indeed not well.

Some time later a photograph appeared on the front cover of *The Bulletin* in Australia showing me, together with psychologist Tim Watson-Monroe, walking Bond across St Georges Terrace in Perth during that hearing. Anyone who looks at the photograph will see that Bond was ill. It is my firm view that he certainly was ill at that time and I am still of the opinion that he was too ill to face trial.

Tim Watson-Monroe dealt with Bond extensively over some months to try to ascertain precisely what was wrong with him and Watson-Monroe came to the conclusion that "Bondy could not run a corner store because of his mental incapacity."

This too generated a huge amount of cynicism among the press. In the end the learned magistrate who heard the committal was of the opinion that there was nothing wrong with Bond and the matter proceeded. That was the end of the "I can't remember" defence. If that defence had been successful Bond would have walked away from everything with no convictions.

As a lawyer you may accept a brief to defend anybody

charged with any crime to the best of your ability without misleading the court. You are not paid to believe your client, just to follow lawful instructions. You are also not paid to necessarily like your client (even though, over the years, there were some I did like and always enjoyed representing).

I am an argumentative person by nature and always enjoyed the challenge of a court room battle. I was at my best when it was "backs to the wall" and there was absolutely nothing to lose. It was then that I came out swinging and keen to see how we would go. "Sydney or the bush", as the saying goes.

Bearing in mind that from time to time the police, government agencies and any other prosecuting authority can be careless with the truth, it became my belief very early on that those making allegations ought be put to their proof and if they could not prove their case then the accused received the benefit of the doubt and "walked". One never tired of hearing those magic words "Not Guilty"!

Alan Bond's real talent lies in employing and surrounding himself with very smart, young people and paying them extraordinarily well so that they stay with him. Nothing bears that out more than the Channel 9 debacle.

Everybody in Australia knows of the late Kerry Packer's famous comment that you only get one Alan Bond in your life. The real story surrounding Bond's takeover of Packer's Channel 9 was related to me by Peter Mitchell, who was one of Bond's 2ICs during the Bell Resources investigations. One afternoon Peter came to the unit where I was staying in Perth and asked me to act for him as well as for Bondy. Of course, I could not act for Peter or for Tony Oates because it would have constituted a potential conflict of interest.

Before I get to the Channel 9 story, I should also point out that Bondy instructed me that Tony Oates, who was the head of finance at Bond Corporation at the time of Bell Resources' takeover, would be able to provide me with evidence that would absolutely absolve Bond of any culpability in relation to the Bell Resources cash strip. Bond gave me instructions to travel to Gdansk in Poland to visit Oates and obtain those instructions, then return to Australia. The timing was not good as I was to travel to Poland a few days before the La Promenade committal was due to begin. This was to be a rushed trip: there and back in six days. It took a long while for Tony Oates even to talk to me on the phone, let alone say that he would provide any evidence whatsoever that could be of assistance to Bond. I eventually got hold of Oates by phone and he finally said he would talk to me, but only in the presence of his Australian solicitor, Mark Webek from Sydney. I had to contact Mr Webek and get his consent, then arrange for both of us to travel to Poland, which we subsequently did.

When we arrived in Poland, it was high summer. Yet the temperature was a chilly 13 degrees Celsius and the rain was whipping across the Gdansk airport parallel to the tarmac.

We had to walk from the plane to the terminal and there-after went to supposedly the best hotel in Gdansk, which was at best two stars and appalling. To make sure that Oates was going to see us, Mark Webek phoned him from Melbourne Airport, then from Singapore and London (where we had to transfer). We then flew to Hamburg and took an Aeroflot flight to Gdansk. Talk about a cook's tour!

When we arrived at Gdansk in the evening, Mark Webek phoned Oates and confirmed our appointment for nine o'clock the next morning as we would have only one day there. The next morning, we travelled to the Elbrewery, Poland's largest brewery, which Oates had purchased and was running, thus gaining himself, at that stage, immunity from extradition to Australia. If we had been able to get the evidence from Oates and make an application to have evidence taken on commission in Poland rather than require Oates to return to Australia, Oates would have been in a position to absolve Bond and he himself wouldn't have been charged with conspiring to defraud Bell Resources, as he eventually was.

We arrived at the Elbrewery the next morning at 9 am. Mark Webek asked to see Mr Oates, with whom we had an appointment. You could have knocked us over with a feather when the receptionist replied, "Mr Oates is not here." What transpired was laughable. It turns out that Oates had been in Gdansk up to the night before, when he had spoken to Webek, and then had changed his mind about seeing us at all. Rather than do us the courtesy of advising us of that, he had left Gdansk and travelled to southern Poland, leaving us high and dry and without the result we had travelled halfway around the world to obtain. We were most unhappy at this. The receptionist said that if we would like to have a look at the brewery we were welcome and Mr Oates had asked that we be given a couple of Elbrewery T-shirts as a souvenir.

Webek was absolutely dumbfounded – even more so than I was, because Oates was his client and had not even bothered to tell him that he wasn't going to be there.

By the time we returned to Australia, the La Promenade committal had begun. Bondy was most excited to hear from me, only to be tragically disappointed when I advised him that Oates had pissed off on the morning we were supposed see him and we had not even spoken one word with him. That was the end of Oates being of any value to us.

Returning to the Channel 9 debacle … Bond had been busting his boiler to purchase Channel 9 and Packer had played him like an old violin. Packer was keen to do the deal man to man – with only Bond and Packer in the room, no other minions at all. Bond, of course, loved the idea of the two heavy hitters being in the same room negotiating a very large transaction.

As the day of the meeting to discuss the sale drew close, Packer placed himself into hospital, ostensibly because he had a crook ticker. All this did was heighten Bond's desire to purchase Channel 9. He waited for the great man to recover and for another meeting to be scheduled.

Mitchell had told me that, on the day of the eventual meeting, he had given Bond very strict instructions not to bid a cent more than a certain figure and waited in another area, along with Bell Group director Peter Beckwith and Finance Director Tony Oates, for Bond and Packer to conclude the negotiations. When all was finished and done, Bondy emerged from the room beaming and said the deal was done.

Mitchell said, "How much Alan?"

"The deal's done. Open the champagne," was all he said.

"Alan, how much?"

"Let's have a glass of champagne. The deal's done. We now own Channel 9."

"Alan, how much?"

"Let's have a champagne."

Then Bond, realising it was pointless to avoid the inevitable, turned around and rather shamefacedly said, "We only paid $ 1 billion." This was some hundreds of millions of dollars more than he was supposed to have paid. Beckwith, Oates and Mitchell, disgusted with Bond's performance, stood up and left.

Of course it is now part of Australian corporate history that, after Bond's financial demise, Packer bought Channel 9 back for about $250 million, thereby sticking a quick $750 million dollars in his pocket after just three years. This is one of the most stunning corporate reverses in this country's history and all brought about by Bondy's ego taking over from his corporate responsibility and that is really the ingredient that landed Bondy in trouble on every occasion.

In relation to La Promenade, he had to have the painting for himself and allowed his ego to take over from any rational examination of the factors. Otherwise, it would have been clearly apparent that to transfer the painting to himself was a theft at best and he shouldn't have done it. The same applies to Bell Resources: his ego took over, particularly in relation to the purchase of the Van Gogh painting Irises, for which he paid almost $54 million, far more than it was worth at the time and using Bell Resources money as well as a loan from the auction house Sotheby's to fund purchase.

Bond made two fatal errors that ultimately brought him down. The first was to sign a personal guarantee at the behest of his mate, Willy Purvis, chairman of the Hong Kong and Shanghai Banking Corporation (HSBC) and the second was to try to take on a bloke called Tiny Rowlands in the attempted takeover of Lonhro (short for London Rhodesia), a mining company in Africa. Rowlands made it his life's work to bring Bond undone because he was of the view that Bond Corporation was, at the time of the attempted raid on Lonhro, technically insolvent – which turns out to have been true. However, that insolvency wouldn't have been any good to Rowlands if Bond hadn't signed the personal guarantee with HSBC. The personal guarantee was then able to be called upon, Bond couldn't pay and Bond was ultimately declared bankrupt as well as going to jail for the Bell Resources and the La Promenade matters. But you can't keep a good man down, as they say: Bondy is now back in action in London endeavouring to get a diamond mine in Lesotho up and running, among other things.

One of the most interesting aspects of all of the Bond transactions were proceedings being conducted by one Richard England, the liquidator of Southern Equities, which was the old Bond Corporation renamed. England is a liquidator of extraordinary persistence. He commenced confidential proceedings against Bond in the Supreme Court of South Australia.

I was in Switzerland when I received a phone call from an Adelaide lawyer telling me that I had to return to Australia immediately. After all the time I'd spent away from home, I had arranged to have a week in Switzerland and then a week in the United Kingdom with my wife. I had not had a holiday for years, due to the Bond proceedings, so I was very reluctant to cancel our plans. "This had better be urgent," I told the lawyer. "Mate, this is bloody urgent," he said. I had to forego my holiday and return to Australia.

I then spent the next few months travelling backwards and forwards to Adelaide where Richard England was vigorously pursuing all avenues available to him to ascertain whether Bond had any money and, if he did, where it had been secreted to. People were brought to Australia from all over the world to give evidence against Bond and thus help to discover where the money was. The big hole in all of this was that Gorg Bolag could not be brought to Australia because there was no mechanism by which Australia could ask for him to be extradited from Switzerland where he had not committed an offence. So as long as Bolag did not come to Australia he could not be interviewed or charged. It transpired that each time I needed to obtain instructions from Bolag he would meet me in Singapore and I flew backwards and forwards to Singapore a few times to obtain instructions.

The most breathtaking part of all of this was the extraordinarily arrogant attitude of Richard England and the people acting on his behalf in pursuing Bond. On one occasion the examining parties were unable to have Bond brought to South Australia as he was a serving prisoner in Western Australia. The proceedings were therefore adjourned holus-bolus to Western Australia. The Supreme Court of South Australia simply adjourned and reconvened at the Carnet Prison Farm, where Bond was then an inmate, with a view to examining him.

My team and I travelled to Perth but did not tell the liquidators' solicitors that there was a hole in their argument to have Bond examined. We all arrived at Carnet – the judge, tipstaff, court officials, liquidators' lawyers, liquidator and Bondy's defence team. We spoke to Bondy and informed him he would not have to give evidence because they had overlooked an important procedural point.

I can still see Alan Bond sitting on a fence outside the

Governor's office where the court convened. The court opened, the judge came in and said "Call Mr Bond", whereupon Tony Howard QC, who was appearing for Bond, informed the court that no Bring Up Order had been signed, therefore Mr Bond was not compelled to give evidence. A Bring Up Order (known in Victoria as a Jail Order) must be signed before someone can be required to give evidence in another jurisdiction. Even though Bondy was in Western Australia, he was being asked to give evidence in the jurisdiction of the Supreme Court of South Australia, which had reconvened there. The liquidators' lawyers had failed to check on the procedures required to force Bond into the stand. When Tony Howard drew his trump card to the attention of the judge, you could have heard a pin drop in the court!

The judge hit the roof and said "Give me a Bring Up Order now and I will sign it and force him to give evidence today." The judge, a justice of the South Australian Supreme Court, was advised that he had no jurisdiction to sign a Western Australian Bring Up Order because it had to be signed by a Western Australian Supreme Court judge. The judge was filthy on this – I don't think I have ever seen a judge as shitty in my life. He then rang the Western Australian Chief Justice and discussed the matter with him. At the end of the discussion, the Chief Justice said he would come and sign the Bring Up Order. Tony Howard then advised the Western Australian judge that the Chief Justice couldn't sign the Bring Up Order either, because it was for the South

Australian jurisdiction; in other words, neither judge had
the power to sign a Bring Up Order which could force Bond,
a prisoner in Western Australia, to give evidence before
a Supreme Court of South Australia in those particular
circumstances. Only a Western Australian Supreme Court
judge could legitimately sign. The result was that the whole
case fell in a hole due to insufficient attention to detail on
the part of the liquidators' lawyers.

The case was over by lunchtime and we set about returning to Melbourne. When we got to the airport we asked where
the liquidators' lawyers were sitting. The booking clerk said
"Don't worry, we've already had a request that you not be
seated within three rows of them!"

The matter subsequently proceeded and took years to
conclude, with the result that I believe Alan's son John
Bond has since settled on a commercial basis with a denial of
liability to the liquidator and Alan has now been discharged
from bankruptcy.

This was an extraordinary period in my professional career
– one in which I travelled around the world non-stop.
Everybody said how lucky I was, travelling all over the world
and flying first class. Yes, in some ways I was, and I generally
stayed in good hotels as well. But when you travel that
much and it's all business and no pleasure it becomes a bit
like catching the bus down the road to work. It is something
that has to be endured. Bear in mind that I used to catch the

Singapore Airlines plane that left Melbourne at twenty to three on a Saturday afternoon and arrive in Zurich at 6.20 on the Sunday morning. I would arrive in Zurich to be greeted by Gorg Bolag and other businessmen suited up and ready for a day's work. They would pick me up from the airport, drive me to the hotel, wait while I had a shower and got changed, and then we would start work immediately. This was not much fun. I worked seven days a week and worked very long hours. I didn't get to see much of Zurich in all the times I travelled there. Yes, I travelled to London and other exciting destinations around the world but the same applied. You were always on a very tight schedule and always bore in mind the fact that you had to be back in Australia quickly either for a court case or in preparation for one.

All of these scenes were flashing through my mind when the cell door opened and I was dragged off to the Melbourne Assessment Prison to start my sentence.

Chapter 4

The Drug Squad – the Enemy Within

A lie travels half way around the world before the
truth has a chance to get its pants on!
MARK TWAIN

This book isn't a general gripe over police corruption, nor am
I asserting that all police are corrupt. But, contrary to what
almost every politician, almost every senior police officer and
the entire Police Association would have you believe, there
has always been, there still is and there will continue to be,
a substantial corrupt element within the Victorian police
force. Most coppers are honest, hardworking, dedicated
law-abiding citizens who take their job seriously and execute
it with a great deal of pride. So I must emphasise that this
chapter is not a slight on all police.

The Victoria Police Drug Squad was formed in the 1970's
and from the outset its brief was to deal, as a specialist unit,

with the growing prevalence of drugs and drug-related crime in the community. Unfortunately, from the outset this specialist squad had some rotten eggs in it.

Prior to the formation of the Drug Squad, the regional crime car squads used to deal with drug matters and the corruption was well and truly entrenched there. I don't know how many times over the years I have been told by a crook that he had been raided by the police, usually the crime cars or the local Criminal Investigation Bureau, and both drugs (or other contraband) and money had been found in the house. Time after time I was told that the coppers would basically look at whatever shouldn't have been there and say "If you forget that [pointing at the money], we will forget this [pointing at the contraband]."

Of course the obvious reaction for any crook is to say "I don't know what you are talking about", and the money would be taken by the police, end of story. No charges would be laid, or if any charges were laid they were minor, indeed, in anyone's language – a cheap way of getting yourself out of a bit of bother.

When the Drug Squad was formed some of these police, who had managed to forge for themselves a bit of a reputation as people who knew what was going on in the drug world, managed to get themselves seconded to the Drug Squad, so right from the outset these same corrupt practices contin-ued. The only variation was that, with more drugs and more money, the rewards for the corrupt police grew.

Additionally there was the question of standover tactics by the police – they would take bribes to turn a blind eye to the conducting of an extremely lucrative industry.

The late Dennis Allen, one of my more notorious clients for some years, was, at the time of his death, on no fewer than eleven sets of bail. A number of those bail applications I considered, before I made them, to be forlorn. However, miraculously something always managed to bob up, often in the form of police giving evidence in private – for him, not against him – which enabled Dennis the Menace to be granted bail yet again. That included one count of murder, during which a police officer gave evidence which, to my mind, was at that time far fetched at best. However improbable it may have been, the evidence was accepted by the judge hearing the application and bail was granted. That officer – Roger Rogerson – was subsequently convicted of corrupt activities in New South Wales and was working in with Victorian police at the time he gave evidence.

His Honour Justice Vincent heard this particular application and as we were leaving his chambers he called Chris Dane QC, who had appeared for Dennis, back and said, "If you expect me to grant this bloke bail again you will need to produce the dingo and the bloke on the grassy knoll!"

When I mention people coming to me reciting the story about drugs and money being found, this was not one or two people over my career; it was hundreds. The story was invariably similar: "We'll forget the drugs if you forget the money." To start with, I didn't believe that the police would behave in this manner but after hearing it repeatedly I began to accept it as probably being correct. Even if 99 per cent of the people who told me this story were lying, it still would have left a substantial number of corrupt instances.

The more the drug industry grew, the bigger the temptation and the bigger the rewards for corrupt activity. It became increasingly easy to skim a quick hundred thousand dollars off the top of the vast quantity of money being found in some drug dealers' houses. Who was going to complain about it? Certainly not the drug dealer, because the coppers were unwittingly doing the crook a favour. If a dealer possessed only a small amount of money it was then open to the defence to say he was a smaller dealer than he may have been thereby resulting in a lesser penalty. The coppers had their pinch, had the drugs, had the tainted proceeds of crime and had some in their own pocket – the classic "win–win" situation.

So it wasn't easy going to court in those days, when I knew that certain members of the force, who were constantly taking the high moral ground, were known to be, or were very likely, corrupt. It also must have been very difficult for the straight coppers to work with these blokes: they would need to have one eye on the crook and one eye on the workmate suspected to be no good.

Stories of drug theft by police became more common and a number of police went to jail for the practice. The most prominent was Kevin Hicks, who was employed at the secure drug facility at Attwood outside Melbourne. The Attwood facility stored all seized drugs awaiting analysis before a case could proceed to court. Hicks, at the request of another old client of mine, the convicted drug dealer Peter Pilarinos, started swapping drugs for other similar-looking substances. One time Hicks swapped red floor tile grout for red phosphorus (an ingredient for cooking methyl amphetamine). You can imagine the bunfight that erupted when the "drugs" were tested and found to be grout. The crook walked, as happy as Larry. Pilarinos had more chemicals to continue "cooking" and Hicks had a few dollars in his kick. Hicks eventually got four years jail for swapping drugs.

A classic example of corruption was the client who was pulled over driving home to the country town where he lived. His car was searched and a six figure amount of cash was found – not a bad pinch. One officer drove the car back to town and, lo and behold, between the time of arrest and arrival at the country station, $35,000 had evaporated. My client hit the roof and it turned out that the copper driving the car was one that Dennis the Menace had previously had on the payroll ... old habits die hard. The client never got the missing dough back, even though he proved to the court that the cash had been legally come by.

Probably the greatest episode of blatant misbehaviour in the Drug Squad came about with the introduction of the "controlled buy" scheme. Detective Senior Sergeant Wayne

Strawhorn came up with this brilliant idea. It entailed police purchasing methyl amphetamine precursor chemicals, such as pseudo ephedrine, from legitimate chemical companies and then, under theoretically strictly controlled environments, selling those chemicals to the underworld with a view to the police then being able to monitor their progression down the line to the ultimate "cook". The police would then swoop and make a clean sweep of the entire amphetamine ring: head man, cook and distributor. A good idea in theory.

These chemicals were not particularly expensive when bought from a legitimate source but in the underworld the same chemicals were always in short supply and hideously expensive. Chemicals that sold illegally for thousands of dollars per kilo cost only a few hundred from the legitimate source. The theory was that none of this product would reach the street – or if it did, it would only be in small amounts and that would be outweighed by the number of crooks who would be caught manufacturing amphetamines.

Things went astray when police started buying additional unspecified amounts of pseudo ephedrine and selling it to criminals without any bookwork or paperwork being done, the very same crooks the police were supposed to later arrest for manufacturing. And they were pocketing a very handy quid along the way. The pharmaceutical companies clearly did not smell a rat as they were still selling to the police they had been told were OK to sell to under the "controlled buy" scheme.

What in heaven's name was going on among the powers that be in the police force at this time? The whole question of controlled purchases was highly controversial, I am informed, but it appears that, once the decision was made to proceed with the scheme, everyone promptly went to sleep at the wheel, thereby enabling shifty business to be done by naughty coppers. Talk about leaving the monkey in charge of the bananas!

What I have been told by more than one crook is that the coppers always had an unlimited supply of pseudo ephedrine but they pulled dirty tricks with the sale of it. On more than one occasion, they made offers that a manufacturer could not refuse. It worked like this.

The police would turn up together at a known cook's house, together with everything required for the manufacture of methyl amphetamine – namely all glassware and chemicals. They would then tell the crook that he was to manufacture amphetamine and there would be a split of the proceeds between the police and the crook and he had the "green light"(ie. full police protection during the cook) to go ahead and manufacture this amphetamine. The Drug Squad would go away and come back at a pre-arranged time in order to collect their proportion of the cook, which one would assume was then sold by the police or sold through crooks on behalf of the police.

The crook would dutifully fulfil his side of the bargain, cooking up the speed. The coppers would return, take theirs, leave his, significantly leave all the equipment required for the cook (which invariably contained residue of that cook) and leave. The sting in the tail was that the coppers then returned to that same crook who had wrongly trusted the police and promptly arrest him for the manufacture of the speed he was in possession of. That is known technically as having your cake and eating it too.

This scenario was related to me on more than one occasion by people who could not have possibly known each other. They did not mix in the same criminal circles and came from various parts of the state, so their chance of ever crossing paths, let alone getting together and concocting a similar tale almost word perfect, was remote. Therefore I accepted the fact that this practice had sprung up.

One really wonders how Strawhorn – who, according to my information, had been corrupt for years – had been able to maintain and extend his corrupt activities together with other officers, such as Detective Sergeant Malcolm Rozenes and Senior Detective Steve Paton, to the extent that he was able to put together such a scheme, get the OK from force command and thereafter proceed to abuse that trust to a mind-boggling degree. Whoever was his superior and whoever was in charge of the police force really has serious questions to answer. Yet the Victorian government simply does not have the political will to follow it up, because they know that, should they conduct a Royal Commission into the police force – that is, a proper unfettered, robust Royal

Commission and not one of those Mickey Mouse show trails that they indulge in – significant and embarrassing matters for the police force and the government would arise from it.

My old client Lewis Moran, somebody I trusted, at one stage confided in me that he had been approached by Strawhorn to "do business" (to purchase precursor chemicals) and asked what I thought. My immediate reaction was not to have a bar of it. Some time later Lewis told me that he had thought about it, decided the offer was too good to refuse, and had taken it up and was doing business with Strawhorn. This was the purchase of pseudo ephedrine from Strawhorn for the purposes of manufacturing methyl amphetamine.

I accepted this as correct because, while discussing that issue, Lewis conveyed to me a message from Strawhorn. That message was that I should stop buying my cocaine from the bloke who drives the gunmetal-grey 7 series BMW. That did rattle me because at that time the driver of that car, Peter Jacobson, was supplying me with cocaine. (Jacobson was eventually charged with use and possess, he slipped off the hook nicely, because the police couldn't find anyone to give evidence against him for trafficking.) Lewis would not have known this: he didn't know Jacobson, nor did his sons, so I was unsettled for a little while because I thought the coppers must be onto me. But then I thought, "Well I'm only using, so what's the problem?" At that stage I didn't know Werner Roberts and I was using fairly regularly, but not to the extent that it was a problem.

You might be wondering how on earth I got to use cocaine in the first place. People often ask me: "How in heaven's name did you fall into drug use to the degree that you became as hopelessly addicted as you were?" I have asked myself the same question and, lame as it may sound, I don't have a complete answer.

I became involved in cocaine use as a social thing on an occasional basis. On reflection, I probably saw using as another trapping of my success. Makes no sense now, does it? Black humour has it that a cocaine habit is God's way of telling you that you have too much money. Believe me, that notion, even if true in the beginning, ceases to apply once you start belting the stuff up your nose to the tune of thousands of dollars per week!

Anyone who says they don't like cocaine has probably never tried it. The greatest danger of the drug is its attractiveness. Cocaine made me feel euphoric, ten feet tall and bullet proof. I have to admit that this was the last thing my personality type needed – more confidence and attitude. I became overbearing (some might say only more so than usual!) and, frankly, a pain in the arse. Many people quietly dropped me – professionally and socially – but it didn't matter to me as long as I had a little bag of powder in my pocket. I did not have any insight into the real reasons people avoided me as I was beyond recall by that point.

Even while I was deluding myself that my use was under control, I was at the same time concerned about where I was heading. Once you realise you have an addiction it is too late because your life, by then, is spiralling out of control. I was impossible to live with and would not listen to anyone who told me so. I am so, so sorry for all the pain I caused my wife. She suffered greatly but stuck by me for as long as she could, until it got the better of her and she could take no more.

Getting back to Lewis Moran, I was wrong-footed by the message he bore from Strawhorn. I knew from that comment alone that the two really were very close and must have been doing business. That was not the sort of operational advice, or information, that would generally be chucked around by the coppers for the fun of it.

Over the next few months, whenever I saw Lewis Moran, I would always enquire as to whether he was doing business with the police. And the answer was always "Yes". I can remember one time when we were standing in the stairwell of the car park at the back on my building and he said that Strawhorn told him to tell me to pull up on the using. Lewis went on to say I was doing too much and because he was my friend he was telling me for my own good. No mention was made of any trafficking at that stage.

You may wonder why we were in the stairwell of the car park. Lewis had a healthy suspicion of being taped or listened to by anyone, so we would walk out of my office into the car park at the back of my building and go and stand in the stairwell, which was concrete. He knew that somebody could still tape him in there, but at least he had taken every possible precaution. This became our habit, so much so that it was referred to as the "cone of silence".

As I said earlier, a number of crooks had come to me telling exactly the same story about doing business with police. But in 1999 matters went up a notch when a couple of lawyers came to me on behalf of their clients. One barrister and one solicitor acting for different clients came to me because of my seniority as a criminal solicitor and the reputation that I enjoyed at that stage as one who knew the law in relation to drug work. Both of these lawyers conveyed the same old story to me: of a client being made an offer he can't refuse by the coppers and thereafter being pinched by the police for manufacture.

The lawyers were unsure what to do. They told me they couldn't possibly go to Victoria Police Ethical Standards, as it was then called (and an oxymoron at that), because there were officers in that squad at the time who had plenty of their own skeletons in the closet and any serious complaint such as this would surely get back to the Drug Squad, creating additional aggravation for the lawyers concerned and their clients.

I foolishly told them I was happy to get involved and that I would talk to somebody in the Victoria Police who I did trust, and I subsequently did that. That officer, who is now no longer in the job, advised me that the best thing to do was take these matters to the National Crime Authority (the NCA). I said it had to be absolutely iron clad that this didn't get out; otherwise there would be all sorts of bother, not only for me but also for the other parties – the lawyers and crooks involved. He assured me this would not happen and gave me the name of a sergeant of the Victorian Police who was on secondment to the NCA, saying I should ring him and give him a preliminary outline of what was going on then seek his advice as to any course of action he thought appropriate.

I rang this policeman at the NCA and explained to him what was going on. I explained that I had the first-hand experience of a number of people having come to me with the same complaint and that now other lawyers had come to me with that complaint too. All of them mentioned Strawhorn as the prime mover and driving force in these corrupt activities.

The officer said he would get back to me about the matter and he would treat the information in the strictest of confidence. I stressed that under no circumstances should this matter be raised with anybody in the Victorian police force because of the drastic consequences it could have for me. I did not hear from him again.

I was like a cat on hot bricks. I had been very uneasy about the course I had adopted and had a feeling of impending doom: I could not have been closer to the mark!

After a couple of days of not hearing back from the NCA officer, I rang him and, to my utter amazement, he advised me that the existing protocol required that he refer the matter to Ethical Standards of the Victoria Police – precisely what I had stipulated was not to take place. I was shocked and I felt sick in the guts because I knew what would happen next.

I said to him, "Why did you do it?" He said, "We don't have the authority to investigate what is a Vic. Pol. internal disciplinary matter. It is part of our charter not to enter into that sort of investigation." If an investigation such as that was to take place, it had to go back to the state. I reaffirmed that I had told him under no circumstances was this to go anywhere but the National Crime Authority and his comment was, "Bad luck, that's the way it's done." As I hung up, I thought "This is going to be fun now…"

I didn't have long to wait. A couple of weeks later I was walking to my office around the corner from the Melbourne Magistrates' Court in Lonsdale Street. I nearly died when I saw, walking up the hill towards me, none other than Detective Senior Sergeant Wayne Strawhorn. I was walking downhill against the building line, he was walking up the hill on the gutter side of the footpath. He looked at me and, pointing two fingers in a pistol-like action, he cocked his thumb at me in a shooting action. He did that with his right hand, then lowered his hand, walked across the footpath to me and said, a few centimetres from my face, "Don't talk out of school." You can imagine the effect that had on me!

Not long after that, all the applications for listening device warrants to install listening devices in my office, car and home were sworn out by the Drug Squad before Justice Barry Beach of the Supreme Court of Victoria.

Of course I played right into the police's hands by managing to have a habit and, further, being stupid enough to get into anti-corruption activity against those who would ultimately have the capacity to bring my life as it was to a screaming halt. I didn't realise the extent to which the police would play dirty, but they certainly did, in spades.

I've never been given a copy of the warrants sworn out by senior police on the intelligence provided by Strawhorn. The applications for the warrants were all made in secret and one wonders what they contain by way of pungent material. I don't question the senior officers who swore the affidavits in support of the applications but I do question what intelligence they received that gave them the basis to swear those affidavits, and a Supreme Court judge to order that the devices be allowed, and the motives of those who provided the intelligence to Strawhorn. After I was charged, the Commonwealth Director of Public Prosecutions resisted all efforts by my representatives for access to the affidavit material. The question of bugging a solicitor's office and the questions of professional privilege have never been addressed. The affidavits would make interesting reading indeed!

If I had been paying close attention to my life at that stage I would have realised that listening devices had been installed in my office. I can remember arriving in my office early one morning to find dust on my table from the acoustic tiles in the ceiling. Somebody had clearly been in and moved the acoustic ceiling tiles overnight, disturbing the dust. The same applied in my boardroom: I should have seen the small hole in the wall over the power point where a device had been placed. But no, although I noted the sloppiness of the work done, I didn't draw the obvious conclusion – I was out of the game by then. Not so out of it, though, that I didn't notice that whoever had placed the listening devices also stole my book *Walsh Street* by Tom Noble about the murders of two young Melbourne policemen.

I subsequently (from jail) made a complaint to the Victoria Police Ethical Standards Department about the handling of this matter by the NCA and I had more than one interview with Ethical Standards. The outcome was zilch. I know that these allegations have never been thoroughly investigated either by the NCA (or their successor the Australian Crime Commission) or by Victoria Police. How do I know? Well, I know firstly that the former officer, who no longer lives in this country, has never been contacted by anybody to ask him about what advice he gave me, secondly that the lawyers concerned have never been contacted by the police about the allegations and thirdly that none of the crooks who had made the allegations to me have been contacted by the police about these matters either.

Just to explain. The Drug Squad as it then was operated in "Crews" which were generally made up of a Detective Senior Sergeant (Strawhorn), a Detective Sergeant (Rozenes) and two or more Senior Detectives (Paton and Firth). As I had reported Strawhorn to the NCA and he had to cover his own backside by "getting" me, he employed like-minded (read corrupt) detectives to carry out the highly secret investigation into me.

Strawhorn had come up with the controlled purchase scheme to sell precursor chemicals to crooks under controlled circumstances. It has now emerged that approximately 80 per cent of those chemicals were never finally accounted for and hence made it onto the streets. This was no small amount, nearly 1 million tablets had been turned into street drugs in one year alone. Well done by all in the force at the time!

Once Strawhorn got wind of my complaints his nice little earner had to be protected, hence "get Fraser". I again accept that my idiotic behaviour gave them a walk-up start to pinch me and I only have myself to blame for my own demise.

After I was charged, however, the lid could not be kept on the rampant corrupt activities of the Drug Squad and it all started to unravel. Paton was charged first with trafficking methyl amphetamine, followed by Rozenes with trafficking ecstasy. Finally the sneakiest and slipperiest, Strawhorn, was charged with trafficking methyl amphetamine. Firth was not charged but suspended, and rather than face the music, retired under a huge cloud.

Other Drug Squad coppers ended up being charged, convicted and jailed for corrupt activities – to such a degree that the squad ended up being disbanded in the mid-2000s. The new drug investigation unit is nothing like the old Drug Squad and should not be tarred with the same brush.

I call for a Royal Commission in this state – not only into the Victoria Police in general but into the corrupt activities of the former Drug Squad in particular. Until this happens, today's honest, hard-working, dedicated coppers will unfortunately wear some of the slur from their no-good mates which must inevitably rub off on them.

As the investigation into me heated up, so did my habit. By that time I had met Werner Roberts, who was introduced to me by another client: he originally instructed me to act in relation to a claim over a back injury he had suffered in the course of his employment. I subsequently negotiated a settlement for him and he received a healthy compensation cheque.

I rang Roberts to see whether he had received the cheque. He told me he had and that we should meet at the Dogs' Bar for a drink to discuss fees. The Dogs' Bar is in St Kilda, not far from where we both lived at the time. I met him and we had a glass of wine and discussed what he owed me. Roberts then went to his bank, obtained the payment and brought it back to the Dogs' Bar. After that we had another glass of wine and decided to leave. As we were leaving he asked me whether I still liked cocaine and I said "Why do you ask that?" He said "Well, the bloke who introduced us told me you don't mind it." I confirmed my liking and Roberts said, "Follow me home. I just live around the corner", which I did. This was the beginning of the end.

Roberts came to the front door and handed me an

envelope which, to my surprise, contained one "rock" weighing approximately a quarter of an ounce of what was clearly very high grade cocaine. He then told me that he and his wife were importers and they sell only in kilos or pounds (drug dealers jump between metric and imperial weight measurements – they sell in grams, ounces, pounds or kilos) but it would always be there for me – that he always had it and he was prepared to make an exception to his rule for me and sell me small amounts for personal use.

As I said, Roberts lived literally around the corner from me, less than a five-minute drive away, and this cocaine was of such good quality that I was soon back knocking on his door. This behaviour gave the police all the ammunition they needed. I was merely a user and any trafficking I could be accused of was what is known in the law as "mates trafficking" – that is, whoever has access to drugs does the purchasing and everybody buys their share. This is technically trafficking but up until I was sentenced, this level of "trafficking" generally did not attract a jail sentence as the purpose of the "traffic" was to share using between friends – there was no commercial element attached.

Things went from bad to worse for me now that I had ready access to high-quality cocaine. I became a regular visitor to Roberts's house and the police tumbled to the fact that Roberts was a substantial trafficker. They started listening to and monitoring his activities, which then also brought the activities of his wife Andrea Mohr and his mate Carl

Urbanec to the attention of the coppers. The inevitable followed: the police were a wakeup to Roberts's importation racket and were conducting substantial surveillance on him and his associates.

It is now a little unclear as to what really took place when Roberts landed in Sydney on his return from Africa. The official line is that Federal and Victorian police watched Roberts exit customs and head south in a hire car. Roberts was followed and arrested when he reached Victoria.

The alternative story, which Roberts sought to raise as his defence, is that the police lost surveillance contact in the early hours after Roberts's return to New South Wales and that now-convicted trafficker Senior Detective Steve Paton met Roberts during that period and gave him the cocaine to bring back to Victoria. This evidence was not allowed by Judge Hart during Roberts's trial because, even though Paton had by this time been charged and had done a deal to plead guilty, he was technically not guilty at the time Roberts wanted to introduce the evidence.

To this day I cannot understand why, if Paton had already done a deal to plead guilty and had admitted his culpability, that very issue couldn't be raised in the defence of Roberts.

On the night the police turned up at my house at 3.35 am, there was no cocaine in the house. Roberts later told me that the police had tried to force him to deliver two kilos to me and they would have raided me afterwards and charged me for that as well. That would surely have been the end of me.

At the time of the raid the police ran through the front door with guns blazing. This was patently absurd as they knew precisely who I was and that I was not violent and would not have a gun in the house. Apart from the massive shock the raid was to me, I jacked up at the sight of all these firearms and told the coppers they couldn't come in, warrant or no warrant, because I had children asleep. A bit of a standoff followed until sanity prevailed and the officer in charge told the police to get rid of their guns. They came back into the house without their firearms and behaved sensibly for the rest of the raid. I concede that the conducting of the search of my house was done very professionally and the next morning my children did not even know that the police had been in the house. They were only young at the time, but you could understand the profound impact that widespread knowledge of this raid has had on them ever since.

I couldn't believe my eyes when I saw Paton and Rozenes in the raid on my house. I knew Rozenes was corrupt; he had been so for a long while. He was known to many barristers to be corrupt and his seizing of the high moral ground was frankly a joke. The late criminal barrister Lilian Leider QC had told me that the reason a good Jewish boy like Rozenes was in the Drug Squad was because he could not afford to leave! Rozenes kept insisting that there was foreign currency in the house. I said yes, there was foreign currency, and showed him my passport. At that time I was a constant overseas traveller, mainly on criminal defence business but also for pleasure. I always kept a couple of hundred Swiss francs, a couple of hundred US dollars and couple of hundred British pounds, so that when I got off the plane at any destination I could get to a hotel or buy a cup of coffee with no mucking around. At the sight of this relatively small amount of money Rozenes was decidedly unhappy and said, "Where's the rest?" I said, "There isn't any more." The police ultimately accepted that there was no foreign currency to speak of and there was no cocaine in the house either as I had used the small amount I had purchased from Roberts's wife the day before the raid. Unfortunately there were two ecstasy tablets found in the top pocket of my suit coat that had been put there by a police plant named Brickell the evening before. But that was that – no huge amounts of anything.

After Paton was convicted of drug trafficking, Paton told *The Age* newspaper that a senior member of the drug squad told him to plant cocaine in Fraser's home before his arrest "as insurance" which he says he refused to do. The senior member of the drug squad was obviously making sure that I was going to be put away.

At the time, though, I was arrested and taken to the Melbourne Custody Centre where the charges were lodged with the charge sergeant. The greeting from the bail justice was rather terse: "Whack him in the cage," he said, "until the bail justice arrives." "The what?" "The cage" was the reply, and he pointed to a number of cages near the counter. There it was – yes, a cage – about one cubic metre of wire mesh.

Even though, as a lawyer, I had visited hundreds of clients held in custody here, I had no idea such "accommodation" existed and was shocked to see it from the outside, let alone from the inside. To say that I had not had a good night was an understatement and being caged up didn't exactly do much to improve matters! I was thoroughly traumatised by the entire experience. Standing in the cage I realised the shit had well and truly hit the fan, as the saying goes, and I was covered in it (metaphorically speaking, of course).

When I look back now to that morning, at least I am able to see a positive in that I figured I had a choice: either clean up my act and profoundly changed my life or it was all over for me and there would be no second chance. The bail justice arrived. I remember shaking like a wet dog, I felt so crook. This was the result of prolonged drug abuse and the trauma of arrest and being caged. I presented my own bail application and bail was granted in relation to use and possess only and one count of mates trafficking.

The uproar within legal circles that followed my arrest was unbelievable. I've seen a few bun fights in my day but I had never seen one like this. The rumour mill went into overdrive and all sorts of outrageous allegations were made about judges and senior members of the profession being caught up in my investigation and about numerous charges that were supposedly to follow, none of which transpired.

Eight years after my arrest and imprisonment the whole saga is still a talking point. While I was drafting this book the issue of lawyers and drug use resurfaced, with the well known Melbourne QC Peter Hayes overdosing on cocaine in an Adelaide hotel and being found unconscious in his underpants with a couple of call girls. Hayes has since died and my thoughts are with his family. The entire week following the tragic demise of Peter Hayes was spent fending off yet another media frenzy seeking my opinion. Hasn't anything interesting happened on this planet in the last eight years?

The legal profession is a microcosm of society – so, as a matter of pure statistics, drug use is prevalent there just as it is in the wider community. All the arse covering, self-justification and general prevarication that goes on does nothing to address the issue. The governing body of lawyers in Victoria, the Law Institute of Victoria, has no effective counselling regime in place and it follows that there is no way any lawyer would feel comfortable coming forward to discuss a substance abuse problem. Over the years I have seen many lawyers, both barristers and solicitors, use all types of drugs and it is an issue to be addressed in a sane and rational manner, not with the hysteria that inevitably follows any one lawyer's exposure for using drugs. I am not naming names because it is all ancient history for me and no good purpose would be served by providing a bit of titillation. As I said earlier, the Law Institute was of no help or support to me immediately after my arrest.

A couple of weeks after my release on bail, I admitted myself to hospital and dried out for eight days. During that time I received intensive psychiatric help and was placed on anti-depressants. While I was feeling better, my life was a complete shambles. I went back to work and the Law Institute immediately made an application to have my practising certificate cancelled, notwithstanding the fact that I had not been convicted of anything let alone sentenced at that stage.

I lasted on the anti-depressants for only one script: the yippee beans were deadening my faculties and I had already come to the most important decision I could on this journey: the only way you stop using drugs is to stop using – no smokescreens, no mirrors, you just stop. Be under no misapprehension, overcoming a drug habit is not easy – in fact, it is bloody hard work – but after seeing the total lack of concrete or successful rehabilitation programmes in jail I am convinced this is the only way to go. I knew that, as a recovering addict, I would come into contact on a daily basis with "triggers" that reminded me of using and that I would need to be ever vigilant. However, it was clear to me that I had got on top of my addiction when, instead of getting a feeling of excited anticipation on encountering one of these triggers, I started to feel revulsion not only at the thought of using but also at what using did to my life. I no longer wanted a bar of it.

Compare and contrast the attitude of the Law Institute to that of the Australian Medical Association. As I have already reflected, if a member of the AMA falls under the grip of drugs he or she is given treatment, counselling and assistance with the conduct of their practice – no suggestion of further destabilising an already fragile person by attempting to deprive them of their livelihood and hold them up to public opprobrium. The member receives as much help as they require to get back on the straight and narrow with minimum impact. Unfortunately the legal profession is rather akin to a bay full of sharks: they feed off each other and have no compassion.

I went back to work and was amazed at the support I got from my clients. Yes, I did lose clients but not the number I thought I would. As a result, I was still in court virtually every day battling away as best I could. It was hard work trying to act professionally and as if all was normal when there was no shortage of professional sniping and backstabbing together with an ever-present fear for my future and, more importantly, that of my wife and children.

I was trying desperately to get on top of this whole mess when Detective Senior Sergeant Wayne Strawhorn rang me and said "I want to see you for coffee downstairs." That was about 5.30 in the evening. I said I couldn't meet him as I was flat out in my office. With that, Strawhorn and a couple of officers from the Australian Federal Police who had charged Werner Roberts, Andrea Mohr and Carl Urbanec with importation arrived in my office. Without further ado I was arrested by the Australian Federal Police, with the ever-smirking Strawhorn and Rozenes present, on a charge of being knowingly concerned with the importation of a commercial quantity of cocaine. The wheels had just fallen off my life!

I was escorted to AFP headquarters where I was held and

interviewed for nearly the whole night. In the early hours of the morning I was placed in the cells of the city watch-house under the Melbourne Magistrates' Court. This was my first night in custody and I did not sleep a wink. During the course of the interviews that night, I told the police all that I knew, which wasn't much, and the AFP were professional in their dealings with me.

I was obviously concerned about being granted bail. If charged with being knowingly concerned with an importation you're only granted bail in exceptional circumstances. The police said that they would not oppose bail and we discussed terms and conditions of the bail that would be consented to by the prosecution, thereby presuming bail to be a done deal.

At the end of the interview, though, when I was about to be lodged in the cells, the AFP said they had changed their mind. "Oh, we will have to formally oppose bail," they said. Now, "formally oppose" usually means that they have no objection to it and that is a sort of a "wink, wink, nod, nod" indication to the court that while the Act obliges them to usually oppose bail they don't really. So even though I wasn't happy, I was placed in the cells and there I remained till the morning. I had to have a suit brought in – but with no belt and no laces in my shoes, and I wasn't allowed to have a shave. My first strip search followed. It is hard to describe the feeling of being strip searched for the first time. It is about as degrading and humiliating an experience as it is possible to have. And don't you think the prison officers I had given a hard time to over the years in witness boxes and interrogations didn't enjoy evening up with me to some small pathetic, infantile degree. I soon learnt that that attitude is par for the course among prison officers.

The strip search is conducted in the strip room, which has absolutely nothing in it so there is nowhere to secrete drugs or contraband. More than one officer comes into the room and the strip commences. Shoes, one at a time, the insoles being pulled out even if they have never been removed before. Then socks, each being minutely searched just in case you have a rocket launcher hidden in one of them! This absurd charade continues with each item of clothing, one at a time, until you are left standing in nothing but your underpants. Then the best bit: drop your undies, lift up your testicles, then turn around, stand with your legs apart, bend over and spread your cheeks which is invariably greeted with the witticism "smile for the Governor". Your clothes are then hurled back at you and you're left to get dressed again. Not a pleasant experience.

The next morning when I was back in my office, Con Heliotis QC was kind enough to visit me with Dr Greg Lyon SC, who, as I said, was a great mate throughout my ordeal. They said that the Crown was hotly opposing my bail. I couldn't believe my ears after all the lies from the night before, but on reflection I should have been expecting the summersault. They further stated that the prosecution had arranged for the magistrate Kevin Mason to hear the bail application and it was a forgone conclusion, on Mason's form, that I would be refused bail. Magistrate shopping was alive and well in Victoria. I was in the depths of despair until Con came and said "Mason isn't going to hear the matter. Another magistrate by the name of Michael Smith is going to hear the matter." Immediately I relaxed, not because His Worship is lenient – far from it – but at least he knows the law and is a fair person.

The court case was called on later in the morning. The court room was jam packed, standing room only. Already I was getting sick of the media attention. So you can imagine how I feel now, writing this book after over eight years of it.

The application was opposed and Con Heliotis did a terrific job of cross-examining the coppers. The prosecutor, Jim Fuller, would not be drawn on the question as to why I should be refused bail. His Worship ended up saying to Fuller, "Give me one good reason why this man should be refused bail" and he couldn't. Rather than answer the question, he ducked and weaved and generally prevaricated, as is usual with the Commonwealth when they are in a corner. His Worship repeated the demand and again Fuller ducked it. His Worship was clearly becoming impatient. He made the demand a third time and when Fuller still couldn't give a sensible response His Worship said, "Sit down. I've heard enough." He said he could not think of one reason why I should be refused bail. I was released on bail to await my fate. I was required to give a surety of $50,000, together with a reporting condition to

South Melbourne Police Station three times weekly and the surrendering of my passport.

I decided to be pro-active as far as my rehabilitation was concerned. I knew it was insufficient to just not use. Apart from my genuine wish to be clean, I would need to prove non-use when my case came up, so I began random drug testing and had counselling with three psychologists to stay away from drugs and patch up my family situation. My then wife was a tower of support and kept life as normal as it could be for me and my children. Since starting random testing before, during and post jail, I am pleased to say I have not returned one "dirty" sample.

In a parallel universe, Roberts, Mohr and Urbanec had all been refused bail and were therefore on remand. Roberts and Urbanec were moved to Port Phillip Prison at Laverton outside Melbourne, which is a privately owned maximum-security facility that features later in my story.

It turns out that Roberts was placed in a unit known as Alexander North. Each of the units at Port Phillip is named after one of the ships in the First Fleet of ships to bring European settlers to this country. Alexander North is a medical unit and Roberts was there with a former client of mine, Mike Juric, who was a gold-plated lunatic and is now deceased.

Juric was a poly drug abuser: it didn't matter what is was as long as he got his hands on it and ingested it in any manner. Apparently Roberts, unbeknown to me, was not only a cocaine user but a heroin user and he scored heroin from

Juric. He promptly overdosed and it was a close call as to whether he would stay with us. He did survive and Rozenes and Firth, from the Drug Squad, went and saw Juric and told him that the overdose was not an accident, it was a direct attempt to kill Roberts instigated by me.

The police then visited Roberts as well and told him that his overdose was not accidental but a deliberate attempt by me to have him killed by Juric, that I had arranged for Juric to be supplied with top quality heroin through some of my ex-clients in jail and that Juric was to be paid to inject the heroin into Roberts and kill him. The whole story was a total fabrication on the part of the police and was not based on any evidence whatsoever. Remember Rozenes, Strawhorn, Paton and Firth were keen to discredit me in any way possible.

Mike Juric had been a client of mine many years before and I knew him to be a lunatic of the first degree. He had the dubious honour of being the only client sacked by me for his behaviour. In one of his amphetamine-induced rages many years ago, he had stopped at some traffic lights, hauled a driver out of his car and flogged him. He then hauled the driver's twelve-year-old son out and gave him a thrashing into the bargain.

As a criminal lawyer, you can cop a lot of things that most people in society may find unpalatable. The test is not whether you agree with what the offender may or may not have done; nor, as I have said, is it your job to judge guilt and / or innocence. I would have acted for Juric if he had only been involved in the fight with the adult male but as far as I was concerned he had overstepped the mark by a country mile in hitting an innocent child to the degree that he did. It wasn't just a hit – it was a thrashing – and the child was badly injured. After that I had no contact with Mike Juric for at least fifteen years, until I went to jail. Hey presto, there he was in the cell next to me at Port Phillip. You can't help bad luck!

As soon as Juric found out I was in the unit he came into my cell and wanted to be my best mate. It is neither easy nor advisable to brush blokes off in jail due to the proximity everyone is to each other, and I was stuck with him sitting on my bed hour after hour pouring out his rantings.

Just to complete the Mike Juric story, his behaviour when I saw him in jail all these years later had not changed one skerrick: he was still a mad drug user who would take anything he could get his hands on in jail. His entire existence in jail revolved around scoring whatever drugs he could from whatever source and consuming them. Juric's view of life was that the more off his face he became, the better – and this is when he became his most obnoxious.

One evening Juric was carrying on like a mug as per usual when another inmate flattened him at the dinner table and a punch-on ensued, with the screws standing back watching until Juric was bashed nearly to a pulp. The screws then called the response "code blue" (a fight) and we were all locked down until Juric was taken off to solitary for being the instigator of the fight. Talk about rough justice!

What had originally landed Juric in jail this time was a particularly nasty torture murder of a helpless old man who Juric and his co-accused wrongly thought had vast amounts of cash in his house. Juric's first trial resulted in a conviction, which he immediately appealed. The appeal was successful and a retrial ordered. After the retrial Juric was amazingly acquitted. Needless to say, once released, Juric got on the "gear" (amphetamines) again, procured a shooter for him-self and was promptly re-arrested for threatening people. His prior history was such that rather than keep him in jail here he was deported from Australia to the old Yugoslavia. I told him before he went that if he kept behaving like this and carrying on like a mug, when he got back to the old country, they wouldn't muck around and somebody would shoot him straight between the eyes.

The joke was that, once the deportation was mooted, Juric panicked. He did not want to go at all. So much for him being the big hard man he tried to portray. When the day of his deportation came he was moved into a suicide cell, placed in a suicide jacket (canvas with Velcro at the shoulder straps so you can't hang yourself) and left for a day. He was not happy and kept the entire unit awake all night in an effort to provoke the screws to such a degree they would give him a belting. No such luck for him. On the morning of Juric's deportation he was forcibly taken from the jail with him kicking and screaming and spitting at the screws – all to no avail. Off he went, and good riddance.

A couple of weeks later the news came back to everyone in jail that, almost straight after being deposited in Croatia, Juric got up to his usual tricks: he scored a substantial amount of drugs, got off his head, bought himself a shooter and got into trouble in a nightclub. He was thrown out and the next night went back with the shooter, and guess what? He was shot straight between the eyes and is now deceased.

To suggest that I had anything to do with Juric, let alone cook up such a half-witted, hair-brained scheme as was alleged, is so far-fetched as to be laughable, but that didn't stop good old Sergeant Rozenes from trying to run it past the court and he gave it as evidence in Roberts's committal. Up until then I had been completely unaware of the existence of any of this. I was told by two barristers who were involved in the committal of Roberts, namely Joe Gullaci, who is now a County Court Judge, and Chris Dane QC, that this evidence had been given and that I should know about it.

That was at the end of the week. On the Saturday afternoon, Steve Butcher from *The Age* rang me asking for a comment on tomorrow's front page lead in *the Sunday Age*. I said I didn't know what the edition was about and Butcher told me that the entire front page was going to consist of a photograph of me together with the headline "Conspiracy to Murder" and the Rozenes evidence was going to be reproduced on the front page.

At that time I was still struggling with all the publicity, struggling with personal problems and struggling with the difficulty of overcoming an addiction. The call from Butcher made me physically ill. This story, if it appeared, was just about the last straw for me and I needed to do something about it. I rang my barrister, Geoff Chettle (now Judge Chettle of the County Court), yet another bloke who really knows how to do his job as a criminal advocate, and to his eternal credit Geoff contacted the magistrate, Rod Crisp. An out-of-sessions sitting of the Melbourne Magistrates' Court was held late on the Saturday evening. His Worship came to the view that the only possible reason for *The Age* running that article was to destroy any credibility I may still have and as it had not been tested under cross-examination of me, he would not allow the article to be published.

I had been deeply disturbed by all of this going on and it indicated to me that my chances of having this case presented fairly by the prosecution or by the police were slim indeed.

I should point out that the Australian Federal Police became involved in this case when it was apparent that the importation by Roberts was going to take place through Sydney Airport and not Melbourne. If it had been through Melbourne then the entire prosecution would have been run by the Victoria Police Drug Squad and I would not have had a hope in Hades of having anything like the true facts presented to the court. The AFP, once they became involved, thought the Victorian police were corrupt and, to their credit told me so; they also believed what I had to tell them.

On one occasion, Senior Detective Firth from the Drug Squad was sitting in on one of my interviews. At that stage I knew that he was being investigated for corruption and he had the temerity to sit in that room and suggest that I wasn't telling the truth. I did my block and told him that he was there because I had consented to him being there, he wasn't part of the interviewing team, and that if he was a smart-arse one more time, there would probably be a fight in the interview room. The Federal Police sent him from the room, came back in and asked me to calm down and said frankly they didn't believe him either and that if I didn't want him back in the room then they would only be too happy to preclude him from the interview. On the understanding that he said not one more word I allowed him to remain in the room. Firth sat quietly, looking chastened, for the remainder of the interview.

It wasn't long after all of this carry-on that I was appearing in a case in Sydney which was to finish the following morning and my client had taken me out for lunch. I was sitting in a restaurant on Sydney Harbour when Greg Lyon rang and told me that Steve Paton had been charged with drug trafficking and corrupt activities. I can remember looking out over the water and being gob-smacked at this prospect. I thought this may have had a positive impact on my case as Paton was the informant in my case. Alas, not so.

Ultimately Paton ended up pleading guilty to drug trafficking and received a sentence of six years with a four-year minimum. Bear in mind the fact that he was a serving police officer, not drug addicted, who conducted these criminal activities purely for personal financial gain. To this day I still cannot work out why he got a year less than I did as an addict who was incidental to a crime, whereas he was the principal offender.

The same applied to Sergeant Rozenes. He was charged with trafficking a substantial amount of ecstasy. I have been informed that, when he was arrested, they threw him to the ground in a park in Caulfield and he immediately indicated to the Ethical Standards officers who were there to conduct the arrest that, in return for a reduced sentence, he would do a deal and tip in every other copper that was involved. As the crooks say, it was a ten slap job: one to start him talking and nine to stop him.

It was known to the authorities prior to my case being heard that Paton and Rozenes had both had these discussions confessing their guilt and had indicated that they would plead guilty. Nevertheless, the Crown prosecutor, Richard Maidment SC, told the court that there was no finding of guilt against either of these people and therefore the evidence of their being charged should not be accepted as evidence before the jury in Robert's case. It's my belief that if the exposure of the corrupt police had been allowed in Roberts' case then the jury could well have come to a very different conclusion that would have had repercussions on my case. Not the least of which was that my case may not have proceeded.

Rozenes subsequently pleaded guilty and, as with Paton, he received a reduced sentence of six years with a four-year minimum. Again he was the principal offender, he was not drug addicted and he committed the offences while a serving police officer purely for financial gain. He was avaricious and had got himself out of his depth financially: that was the catalyst for him committing these offences.

These cases are classic examples of why there should be frank plea bargains in Victoria. If I had been able to properly plea-bargain and been given the indication that I was to receive the sentence I did, then I would have been better off pleading not guilty, fighting the case and taking my chances with the jury. I was handed the same sentence as Mohr and Urbanec, who pleaded not guilty. I thereby received no discount at all for pleading guilty, as is required by the law, and if you read the decision of the Court of Criminal Appeal it is apparent that they refused to reduce my sentence only because I was a lawyer and had brought disgrace upon the profession.

One of the people who made the allegation about corrupt Drug Squad activities was an old client of mine, Bob Slusarczyk, who, sadly, is now dead, so I'm able to talk about it. His allegation was that the Drug Squad arrived with all the necessaries to manufacture amphetamine and told him that was what he was to do. He subsequently did manufacture the amphetamine but the police took the lot this time, leaving him with no rewards for his efforts. When they came back to arrest him for manufacture, they of course found all the equipment with residue from the manufacture in his shed.

This man was a builder of ultra light aircraft and had been one of the first in this country to ever build one. Bob was meticulous in his preparation for the building of the planes and was equally meticulous in his operation of them.

In addition it is clear that he had been loaded by the police – that is, something that wasn't his was placed in his house. He had a reclining rocker and somebody had stuffed a bag of amphetamine in the springs. If you had sat in the chair and reclined, the bag would have torn. The police went into his house, went straight to the chair and pulled the bag out of the springs and said "Look what we've found. This is obviously part of your manufacture." The only catch to that was that when the substance was analysed it was completely different from the amphetamine that had been in Slusarczyk's shed. Just before he was due to give evidence, his ultra light mysteriously fell out of the sky and he was killed. What a surprise.

The corruption within the Drug Squad didn't stop with Paton and Rozenes and Strawhorn: other officers from the Drug Squad were charged and some have now been convicted of very serious offences. One, by the name of Michel, is serving a substantial double-figure sentence for his role in drug trafficking and theft.

While it was not a substantial proportion of the Drug Squad that was charged with corruption, it was certainly an alarming number and again I say there must be a Royal

Commission into the Drug Squad to get to the bottom of what was going on. Somebody must have been asleep at the wheel for this sort of endemic corruption to have been able to take root and flourish.

Fortunately, the Drug Squad has now been disbanded because of all the naughty goings-on – in itself an admission that the concept of a specialist Drug Squad hadn't worked because insufficient vetting of the members had taken place. There is now a new specialist drug investigation unit manned by police I've known for many years and who, as far as I am concerned, are not capable of being corrupted.

Let's hope this state of affairs continues. Otherwise how can any member of our society have confidence in those who, according to the police motto, "uphold the right".

Chapter 5

Keep Your Friends Close and Your Enemies Closer

If you can keep your head when all about you
Are losing theirs and blaming it on you;
If you can trust yourself when all men doubt you,
But make allowances for their doubting too;

IF, RUDYARD KIPLING

Tim Watson-Munro and I had been very close mates for many years, having first met when he came to Melbourne from Sydney. Watson-Munro was a practising clinical forensic psychologist and I came across him regularly in the course of my work. These days it is almost inevitable that you send a person accused of serious offences to a forensic psychologist for assessment before his court case. A defence lawyer needs to ascertain a client's IQ, his ability to distinguish right from wrong, his mental state, whether there are indications of any mental disease. In the case of the latter, the client is referred to a forensic psychiatrist. The long and short of it is that expert witnesses such as Watson-Munro are now an integral cog in the sentencing process in any criminal court in this country.

After I got to know Watson-Munro professionally we socialised on the odd occasion, having lunch or a coffee. I invited him on one occasion to a luncheon get-together I used to have with other people – not only lawyers but people from all walks of life, including judges, politicians, doctors and anyone else considered to be interesting. It was an eclectic group and we had a good time. I was still only using cocaine very occasionally but I had secretively used it at these lunches on more than one occasion, without others being aware of it. One day Watson-Munro approached me and started talking about the use of cocaine. He told me he had been using for years and had an inkling that I might be having a bit of a go at it myself. Watson-Munro offered me some cocaine that he had with him. I partook of what he had offered and that was the beginning of a very close cocaine-related relationship between us that lasted until the time of my arrest. Watson-Munro received all of the psychologists' work from my firms and he would be called to give expert evidence in court. He was a very good witness in those days, so he was always in court.

Lunches became more frequent. We would often meet for a drink after work and the whole system surrounding the use of drugs and the movement of drugs between us was on a mates basis – that is, if he had some, he would share it with me; if I had some, I would share it with him.

Any "trafficking" between Watson-Munro and me was on this basis and happened occasionally, not regularly. In my case I would have sold him only a few grams over a few years and he would have sold me about the same amount.

Our mutual usage continued and Watson-Munro and I saw each other on an almost daily basis. Our friendship was based on three ingredients: mutual use, comfort in the other's company, and an ability to use to our hearts' content as long as we were together and we both possessed sufficient for us to use.

While both Watson-Munro and I were under surveillance by the police I briefed him in a case of a bloke called John Brickell. Unbeknown to me, Brickell was a police plant to try to entrap me into trafficking cocaine to him. In return Brickell did, over a period of time, supply me with a few grams of cocaine, all of this with the full knowledge of the police.

Brickell had been acquitted of a double murder in Sydney. That was not the end of his problems: he had travelled to Melbourne and ended up facing armed robbery charges. These charges mysteriously went away after I was charged and his part in my arrest was made known to the court.

The day before my arrest I appeared for Brickell at the Frankston Magistrate's Court on pistol possession charges. With Brickell's priors he was a certainty to cop a jail sentence. Brickell pleaded guilty and I presented his plea in mitigation.

At the conclusion of the plea, much to my surprise, Brickell was fined $5000, with no jail. I nearly fell over and was pretty chuffed with the result. This result has, upon reflection, worried me over the ensuing years. Was the extraordinary result achieved by my "brilliant" advocacy? I think it was because Brickell was working under cover for the police and it was vital he not be imprisoned. We will never know the answer but I have been uneasy about this result for years.

Brickell was ecstatic at the result and invited me for a beer at a Port Melbourne hotel known to the locals as "the House of Twisted Faces" because of all the crooks that drink there. While at the pub, Brickell asked me if I would like a couple of ecstasy tablets. "No thanks, John," I said, "I don't use them." Regardless, Brickell poked a small plastic bag in the lapel pocket of my suit. When I got home I saw there were a couple of ecstasy tabs in the bag. I was going to flush them but I forgot. That was how I came to be charged with possession of ecstasy. My house was raided early the next morning. What a coincidence.

It just goes to show that drug addiction can lead you to make extremely unsound judgements as to good character. Watson-Munro had been misbehaving himself professionally for years but none of this came to my notice until after I was arrested.

In 1998 Watson-Munro was charged with professional offences relating to improper behaviour with a doctor client that my firm had referred to him. The client was suffering some psychiatric problems and Watson-Munro took advantage of her sexually, which blew out into an affair. Watson-Munro denied this to his solicitors but admitted the affair to me. The affair had continued unabated for some time and on one particular occasion, he and the doctor had a day's outing together. It was the weekend of the Grand Prix Formula 1 motor car race in Melbourne and later Watson-Munro asked me to provide an alibi for him by saying that he had been with me at a party at Peter Jacobson's house after the race. There was only one catch to that idea: there was no party at Jacobson's house on that day. Everybody, including Jacobson, had left the Grand Prix and returned to my house, where I was assigned to babysitting duties while my wife and her friends went to the John Farnham concert.

The doctor subsequently made allegations of professional misconduct against Watson-Munro to the Psychologists Registration Board. He was professionally insured and was referred to Phillips Fox solicitors to act on his behalf. They in turn briefed now County Court Judge Liz Gaynor and Supreme Court Judge Robert Redlich QC to appear for Watson-Munro. The instructions he gave both solicitors and barristers were that he had been at a party at Peter Jacobson's house with me and that I would give that evidence to the Psychologists Registration Board. Liz Gaynor spoke to me on a number of occasions regarding the alibi Watson-Munro had instructed her I would provide. I ducked the issue for as long as I possibly could.

Liz Gaynor, doing her job properly, became so persistent

that one night at my house I had to pull Watson-Munro aside. I took him outside to the backyard and told him that although we were mates I refused to give false evidence and that he would have to look elsewhere if he wanted to pursue those instructions to his counsel. Apparently Watson-Munro didn't change his instructions as Liz Gaynor kept ringing me. One morning I was standing on the steps of the Melbourne Magistrates' Court when she rang yet again. I was finally placed in a position where I had to be brutally frank with her and I said : "Liz you must understand the reason I have been avoiding making a statement for you or giving evidence for Tim." She replied, "What's that?" I said, "The whole thing is a lie, there was no party at Jacobson's and he [Jacobson] was at my house after the Grand Prix." That was the last I heard from Liz Gaynor about the matter.

A little while later, however, on a visit to my house Jacobson raised the question of an alibi. I warned Jacobson that giving evidence of this type was fraught with danger and he could be charged with perjury. Nevertheless he seemed prepared to do it.

On 8 February 1999 the Psychologists Registration Board reprimanded Watson-Munro, having found him guilty of two counts of professional misconduct dating back to 1995.

After I was arrested and with his credibility already on the line, Watson-Munro could scarcely afford to be discredited further and it is my belief that to protect himself and mini-mise the damage to his professional and personal life he was induced to turn Crown witness. He testified against me and said that I was his main supplier of cocaine when the fact was that we supplied one another on a "mates" basis.

Watson-Munro gave evidence at my committal (which was not included in the statement of facts that was later agreed with the Crown) that substantially revolved around a discussion we had on the telephone in which Watson-Munro rang me and said he was going to play footy, which was our code for him going to see a supplier, whom we nicknamed "the Ruckman" due to his size.

I distinctly remember this call, not only because I refreshed my memory by reading the transcript again but because I can distinctly remember Watson-Munro saying he was at the Ruckman's and it was his shout, which meant that he would purchase cocaine for me. I declined and the part that was never put forward in evidence was that the conversation finishes with me replying, "No Tim, I'm trying to pull up." In other words, I told him I was trying to reduce my intake and give the coke away. That piece of evidence is clear to anybody who listens to the tape but it was never produced in court. Either the Crown deliberately didn't lead that evidence so as to paint a different picture of the realities or didn't bother to listen to the relevant tapes before producing them as evidence.

There was another occasion in my office that I distinctly remember and it is on the telephone logs as well. Watson-Munro was treating a now deceased client of mine by the name of Geoffery Harris. Watson-Munro rang me at my office after hours, said he was seeing Harris and did I "want any"? I replied, "Yes, get me a couple." A short while later Watson-Munro arrived outside my office and rang me on my mobile phone. I went downstairs, opened the door and purchased two grams of cocaine from him for $500.

The Psychologists Registration Board were to see a lot more of Watson-Munro as a consequence of his cocaine habit being revealed after my arrest. They became singularly unimpressed with his honesty, no doubt when they realised that at the time they reprimanded him in 1999 Watson-Munro was also using and abusing cocaine on a regular basis.

In June 2000 they declined his registration application and said "his [Watson-Munro's] motivation during his criminal and compromising behaviour over the period of years appears to have been insightless self-gratification." They declined his registration again in 2002 saying, "… his answers continued to be equivocal and evasive. Moreover, in some important aspects he lacked real insight." They concluded that, "he has deceived the Board twice within the last four years. He has sustained a double life for a series of years that not only was deceitful … but involved sustained and serious ethical impropriety … boundaries were crossed, deception was engaged in and sound judgement was not exercised." In 2004 he regained registration but under strict conditions that included working under supervision for a period of two years.

Senior Detective Firth of the Drug Squad, who was later

suspended from the police force, gave sworn evidence to the Psychologists Registration Board in support of Watson-Munro that I was Watson-Munro's main cocaine supplier. Firth gave his evidence to the Board after my case was completed and therefore it follows that the agreed statement of facts in my case was a public document. The agreed statement of facts contradicted Firth's statements but he was not questioned about the agreed facts. It is obvious that the Psychologists Registration Board did not know, and were not told, the real facts.

The circle is thereby complete: you scratch my back, I'll scratch yours. Watson-Munro gave that evidence and Firth helped him out of a tight spot, thereby assisting him to be re-registered as a psychologist and he is back practising as such in Melbourne.

Finally, a small time dealer, Barry Kemp, was also convicted of trafficking to Watson-Munro and me. No mention was ever made of that before the Psychologists Registration Board, nor was mention made of it in my case. Watson-Munro was the one who took me to Kemp's house.

When the music stopped I was left without a chair and was subsequently charged. Before my case had come before the court I was discussing Watson-Munro's statement with Jason and Mark Moran. They had both been psychologically assessed by Watson-Munro and were extraordinarily distressed at the prospect of him being a Crown witness. The obvious implication for them was that, if Watson-Munro had told on me in regard to my social habits, it was highly likely that he would tell on them as he had sensitive material about the brothers' activities which they considered privileged. They left our meeting very unhappy.

A few days later I met them in a coffee shop in town where they asked about Watson-Munro and whether I was of the view that he would actually give evidence. I said I thought that, according to information I had, he would give evidence. Jason and Mark said that they couldn't possibly allow that to happen because any evidence given by Watson-Munro would land them in trouble. Jason said there was only one way to deal with that and that was to go to Watson-Munro's offices and kill him there and then. I told them both to "pull up" – apart from the obvious illegality, there would be disastrous consequences for me if the main Crown witness in my case was killed. Mark pulled back the jacket he was wearing and showed me a pistol stuck in his belt. I was somewhat surprised at this radical change of direction for the two boys and I talked them out of it. I had known both Moran brothers since they were boys and I took this threat very seriously, as both were well and truly capable of carrying it out.

Chapter 6

The Walsh Street Murders

Andrew Fraser is a good tough criminal solicitor. It isn't an easy job. In the mid nineteen eighties one of his better known clients was Dennis Allen, the sort of client that can involve a lawyer in a lot of extra work. Fraser also made himself available to Allen at all hours if legal matters were necessary – such as early morning police raids, and there were plenty of those. Fraser also acted for Peter Allen, Dennis's brother.

Through the nineteen eighties, Fraser gained more experience and skill. His knowledge of how the police operated, with clients like Dennis and Peter, was as good as Melbourne offered. He also knew what legal advice to give his clients and in what circumstances.

WALSH STREET, TOM NOBLE

Building a successful practice is not all about being great as a lawyer or an advocate. A lot of luck is also involved and I have been fortunate enough to have had my fair share of this. I have been in the right place at the right time and have been able to capitalise on those pieces of luck.

Occasionally a big client would appear out of the proverbial woodwork, with no warning. Those clients came to you because they had made up their own minds about you and had decided that you were the lawyer for them. Inevitably they were the clients who stayed through thick and thin. On the other hand there were the clients you had wooed to leave their previous lawyers and come to you. These clients tended to be fickle, if they had jumped ship to come to you then, in turn, they would have no compunction in changing mouthpieces again when and if it suited.

Dennis Allen was one client who just lobbed in my waiting room one day with his mother, Kath Pettingill. Dennis had a couple of mates who had recommended me to act for him and, as he was dissatisfied with his current representation, he instructed me to act. Dennis also placed me on a retainer, which is a fee paid in advance to guarantee his access to me at any time, and in Dennis's case that meant any time!

At that time I didn't have the faintest idea who Dennis was. He had been in a bit of bother and had done a bit of "boob" (jail) but he was nothing out of the ordinary as far as clients went at that time. Dennis had priors ranging from assault and other assorted misbehaviour to a rape – fairly standard for a street lout from Frankston. Little did I realise that Dennis the Menace was about to hit the big time – and how!

Dennis was the founder and driving force behind a large heroin trafficking operation he operated from his home in Stephenson Street, Richmond, an inner Melbourne working class suburb, where he owned several houses. He was a violent and dangerous man and many murders, allegedly carried out by way of enforcing the business, have been attributed to him. My calculation is that Dennis probably killed more than ten people by his own hand. He was a huge drinker and a huge consumer of amphetamine, a product that he preferred to use himself rather than sell. Some say the coppers were his undoing. But in the long run it was his excessive use of the "Lou Reed" (speed), together with his amazing consumption of Jim Beam Bourbon. He was ruthless in the sale of his heroin and he was equally ruthless in collecting the dough, employing violent and dangerous men such as his brother Victor Peirce (now deceased) and the standover man Victor Gouroff.

Things really hotted up for Dennis when he hit the big time. Not being renowned for his subtlety, he soon managed to draw a lot of heat from the police and others in the heroin industry. He needed muscle and he always paid for me to defend them.

One Saturday night I met Victor Gouroff when he was under arrest at the Collingwood Police Station. It was always very confrontational turning up in the lion's den late at night when your client had been in a blue with the constabulary and this night was no exception. I was shown into an interview room where Gouroff was sitting. He was covered in blood and a large cut followed his lower jaw line where he had clearly been kicked. This wound was bleeding profusely.

At one stage during the interview the investigating police left the room to follow up on something and placed a very junior constable in to watch us. He looked like a fish out of water and was clearly apprehensive. Victor started wiping the blood from his jaw and flicking it over the constable, who sat there like a statue. While flicking the blood Victor started singing: "I'll sing you a song and it won't take long…. All coppers are cunts! Second verse, a little bit louder and a little bit worse… All coppers are cunts!" By the time the investigating police returned the poor young copper was covered in blood and was as white as a ghost. I was immediately chucked out of the station and Victor copped another belting for his troubles!

After I had been acting for Dennis for a while he started asking me to act for other members of his family and some of his henchmen who landed themselves in bother. Dennis always paid for my services for these other people. There was always plenty of action around Dennis, trouble followed him around like a bad smell.

Acting for Dennis and all his friends and relations was almost a fulltime job for a good couple of years. It made life pretty hectic but occasionally provided some light relief. One time Dennis was having trouble with a money lender in Richmond because he kept imposing late payment penalties. Dennis did not like the concept of penalties at all. In order to solve the problem he went to the lender's office with a shovel and advised the bloke that he had brought the shovel for the bloke to dig his own grave with if he didn't agree to waive the penalties. Problem solved: no penalties were applied.

The family used the Cherry Tree Hotel and The Wayside Inn, both close to the houses Dennis used to store guns, money and drugs. On one occasion Dennis and a group of crooks were at The Wayside Inn drinking and watching a band. Dennis was a mad Bob Marley fan and kept yelling out to play Bob Marley. The band ignored him until they took a break and the singer went to the toilet. While standing at the urinal Dennis entered the toilet, took out a gun, stuck it at the singer's head and said: "Play Bob Marley or you are off!" Needless to say, the band kicked off the next bracket with Bob Marley!

Dennis the Menace (or "Mr T") as he preferred to be called after the TV character) also had a very handy side business in selling firearms to the underworld and accordingly Dennis always had ready access to firearms.

On one afternoon when I visited Stephenson Street (I always had to go to his house to see him because of his amphetamine psychosis; in the end he refused to even leave his house), Dennis was sitting in the lounge room when he pointed to the Bryant and May clock tower and said, "The bastards have a watching post up there." With that, much to my amazement Dennis produced a handgun, raced out the backdoor and let go about four shots into the clock tower. I couldn't believe my eyes as he calmly walked back in, put the gun down and continued the conversation as if nothing had happened. It was time for me to leave and I did so in some haste.

Dennis was also aware that the police regularly manned a watching post in the old Rosella tomato sauce factory at the end of Stephenson Street. Again, one night as I was leaving his house, he was raving incoherently about the coppers watching him from the Rosella factory, whereupon he went back into one of his other houses and produced an AK47 machine gun. That was it for me – I was off. But before I could go, Dennis let a burst off out of the AK47 down Stephenson Street into the front of the Rosella factory. Anybody who doesn't believe that this happened can go down there to this day and see the pockmarks from the bullets at the front of the factory.

Peter Allen, one of Dennis's brothers, was released from prison and while on parole set up his own business as a substantial heroin trafficker. Peter came unstuck by acquiring for himself a large speed habit and making a practice of raving on about his business, and his plans to take over the world, in his house, where police had installed listening devices.

I first met Peter when he was extradited from New South Wales to face numerous charges in Victoria. He was particularly concerned about returning to New South Wales because he had "bronzed " his cell before leaving. Peter has not learnt a thing from all his sentences and is still in the prison system in Victoria for drug and violence offences.

There were other brothers: Jamie, now deceased; Victor Peirce, also deceased; and Trevor Pettingill, who is still with us and has been extremely quiet since his acquittal over the notorious Walsh Street murders.

Jamie was quite a handful. The first time I met him was at the city watch-house, where he was to face charges of armed robbery. The door to the watch-house flew open and in came a tumbling, fighting, cursing bundle of Jamie and about half a dozen coppers, all struggling to control him. Jamie screamed to get their hands off him because he had hepatitis. The coppers all let him go and one asked how he contracted the disease. "Eating the turds out of the dunny at the Fitzroy cells" came the reply!

Victor Peirce tended to run his own race but did work for Dennis from time to time in the heroin distribution business. Trevor Pettingill also worked for Dennis.

Dennis's house was constantly raided by the police and virtually every second morning on my way to my office, I would have to detour to his place to supervise an early morning raid. It got to the stage that Dennis did not even bother nailing the carpet back down after the raids.

The coppers became suspicious of my constant attendance at these raids and, after a number of them, I too was searched, the police using the excuse that Dennis had probably given me drugs to secrete or dispose of, which was utter nonsense. I was there purely in my capacity as a lawyer and they did not find anything on me.

Dennis had a very wide network of informers and protection and had a number of police in his pay. On one occasion I saw Dennis hand a now ex-detective a brown paper envelope. Dennis said to me "What do you reckon's in there?" I replied, "Obviously dough." He said, "Yes, but how much?" I said "No idea." Dennis replied, "$14,000." This was in the 1980s, when $14,000 was a sizeable amount of money. I said, "Why $14,000? It's an odd amount." He said, "No, it's not. $1000 each per day for him and the other bloke for a week." In other words, Dennis had two coppers on the payroll to the tune of a thousand dollars each per day. I know for a fact that these coppers were friendly to Dennis because he had given me two telephone numbers, along with the instruction that whenever he was arrested, at no matter what time of the day or night, all I had to do was ring one of those two numbers and an unidentified male voice would answer. All I had to say was, "That bloke [meaning Dennis] is at [such and such] Police Station" and hang up. Lo and behold, one of the two police would turn up to supervise the processing of Dennis and invariably he was granted bail.

When Dennis died, the wheels fell off the entire empire because the police pressure had made it difficult for him to retail his drugs as he had liked. And there was no one else who was sufficiently ruthless to continue with the heroin distribution racket on that scale.

Dennis, while being a ruthless killer, was also quite a character, with quite a distinctive appearance. Picture a skinny person covered – and I mean covered – from head to toe in jail tattoos and professional tattoos, wearing (back in the 1980s) over $300,000 worth of gold jewellery, which made Mr T from the television series look like a second-rater. In addition he wore Dunlop Volley runners with the tongues cut out and no laces, no socks, jeans, a blue working man's Jackie Howe singlet and his lucky sports coat. Dennis always wore this coat to court and while he had me appear and he wore the coat he said he was lucky. The proof of that luck was that he had never been convicted. Add to that a mullet hair cut and you have some idea of the image he presented.

It didn't matter which court he was in, he refused to wear anything but that outfit on the basis that he would always be successful. One of the other things that Dennis was obsessed about was making sure his cases never came to hearing. As a result I was paid time and time and time again to go to court and seek adjournments. Most of the time I was success-ful. One application that was not successful springs to mind easily. Dennis had to front the Coroner's Court in relation to the death of a woman by the name of Helga Wagnegg, who had died of a heroin overdose in the backyard of one of Dennis's properties which mum, Kath Pettingill, was using as a brothel and doubled as a front for distributing Dennis' heroin. Dennis told me he tried unsuccessfully to revive her by injecting speed into her jugular vein and when that didn't work he disposed of her body by throwing her in the Yarra River. Dennis knew he was in bother over this and would have some very difficult questions to answer at the Coroner's Court. I don't know how many times I managed to have the Coroner's inquest adjourned until we reached the stage where the Coroner said, "This case is going on, irrespective of what happens."

I spoke to Dennis the night before the inquest and he said to me, "Don't worry, there will be no inquest tomorrow." I begged to differ and Dennis said, "We'll see." The next morning Dennis came to my office before court and reiterated that the inquest would be adjourned. I said that was not possible at this late stage. We drove to the Coroner's Court to find that the place had been fire bombed. I couldn't believe my eyes. Dennis looked at me, smirked and said, "I told you that this case would be adjourned." Needless to say, the Wagnegg matter was finally dealt with and a verdict of death by misadventure was returned. That was in May 1985.

As Dennis became a bigger player and his heroin empire expanded I became extremely busy. I met and acted for many of Melbourne's heaviest and dangerous men such as Victor Pierce, Ross Franklin and Peter Robinson, who at that time was already on parole for murder and was charged with further firearms offences. The list goes on and expanded to numerous Painters and Dockers.

While not acting for all Pierce's mates I met many of them, one of whom was Graeme Jensen.

Graeme Jensen was a well known criminal figure who had convictions for armed robbery and the police were certain he had been involved in other armed robberies, including the robbery / murder of an Armaguard employee by the name of Dominic Hefti. It turns out now that Peirce had nothing to do with that armed robbery. A man by the name of Santo Mercuri was charged and convicted of that murder and I acted for Mercuri in the murder trial. The allegation that never came to trial was that Mark Moran was the other shooter with Mercuri. However, notwithstanding what ultimately transpired, the coppers were sure that Jensen had been involved not only in this armed robbery but also in others.

On 11 October 1988, at about 3.30 in the afternoon, Jensen had travelled from his home to a lawnmower shop in Narre Warren in Melbourne's outer eastern suburbs where, he had told his wife, he was going to purchase a new spark plug for his lawnmower. Jensen was under constant observation by the coppers and, according to one version of events, as he left Narre Warren on that afternoon, he was pulled over by members of the Armed Robbery Squad (which, along with the Drug Squad, has now been disbanded following improper behaviour). The Armed Robbery Squad stated that Jensen produced a firearm, a sawn-off .22 rifle, and pointed it at police, whereupon he was shot dead on the spot by the police.

This was a hugely contentious "attempted arrest" and many in the underworld were firmly of the view that, because the police had been unable to charge Jensen with anything, they'd indulged in a summary execution to get a nuisance out of the way. The police have since made all sorts of allegations about what transpired but the upshot of it is that, unfortunately, on the following night, 12 October 1988, at about 4.47 am, two young, inexperienced coppers, 22-year-old, Steven Tynan and 20-year-old Damian Eyre drove to Walsh Street in South Yarra, an affluent inner Melbourne suburb, to investigate a "parked" Commodore. The vehicle was stationery in the middle of Walsh Street, its doors open and lights on, apparently deserted. The two police began checking the car and while they were doing so they were executed.

They had driven into Walsh Street and parked a short distance behind the white Commodore. It appears from the coroner's inquest that Tynan was sitting in the driver's seat when he was shot in the head with an SG (a single ball, not filled with shot) shotgun. The shotgun was fired from about a metre away. Another shotgun blast hit Constable Eyre across his back. It appeared, on reconstruction, that Eyre had been squatting down next to the open driver's door of the car, probably next to Tynan, inspecting the vehicle. Surprisingly Eyre was able to get up and grapple with one of the gunmen but the other gunman had grabbed the service revolver from Eyre's holster and shot him in the head from point-blank range. Eyre was then shot in the back, again from almost point-blank range.

It is clear that there were at least two shooters involved. It appears that these two policemen were killed for no reason other than that they were police. The killing appeared to be a trap for police, and whoever was unlucky enough to attend the call on that morning was going to lose their lives.

The witnesses, who were few, said they saw two men run-ning away. At the trial of the men subsequently charged with the Walsh Street killings, the Crown alleged that there were five men at the scene: one Jed Horton, Victor Peirce, Peter McEvoy, Trevor Pettingill (Victor's half brother) and a young bloke called Anthony Farrell. I did not know Horton but I had acted for all of the others over the years and it turned out I had a substantial part to play in the subsequent trial.

Following the tragic deaths of these two young police all hell broke loose. Melbourne's underworld and its relationship with the police was changed forever. The police unleashed a reign of terror on the underworld. There was a constant and concentrated smashing down of doors, raiding of premises, arresting of people, bashings, threats and anything else the police could think of to try to rattle the entire underworld with a view to having somebody get the wobbles sufficiently to then give information about who may have been involved in this execution. As things started to happen and police began to figure out who they thought had been involved, the house in which Victor Peirce was living at Chestnut Street, Richmond was, in an extraordinary move, demolished to the very ground looking for the firearm. Nothing was found.

The first person arrested over Walsh Street was one Jason Ryan. He was Dennis Allen's nephew and had been living at Chestnut Street with Victor Peirce and his wife, Wendy (known as Wendy the Witch). Jason was a young lout of the first order who had been Uncle Dennis's delivery boy. Dennis had worked out that it was highly unlikely that the police would suspect a kid as a courier. Dennis was right and Jason left school. He was provided with a new bike and lots of cash to go into the heroin delivery business. I think Jason was thirteen when he went into business.

My then partner Charlie Nikakis was called to Chestnut Street when the police arrived to arrest Jason. Charlie was not allowed to talk to Jason and only saw him being carted away covered in blood by members of the Ty-Eyre Task Force (a task force formed to investigate the Walsh Street murders). That was the last time we saw Jason Ryan before he gave evidence in court. Jason ended up being essentially the only witness for the prosecution and, as he had changed his story more times than you change your socks, he was not even remotely believed.

In his first version Ryan nominated the five who he said were present at Walsh Street during the murders. The police then set about trying to track them all down.

I was aware that I would come under observation, having acted for four of these men, and one evening when I got home from work, I was driving my car into my back yard from the back lane when the old Greek bloke who lived on the lane said to me, "I saw the plumbers at your house today." The only problem was that I hadn't asked for any plumbers to be at my house on that day.

I said, "How many?" He said, "Three, they were in a van

with no signs on the side." I said, "Oh, thanks very much for that." I knew then that my house had been bugged and that my phone was probably being listened to as well. The police were trying to obtain some sort of intelligence from me, should anybody ring me seeking professional advice. They didn't have to wait long. Peter McEvoy rang me and, after a brief discussion, he decided to give himself up as, on his own account, he had nothing to do with the matter.

The event that changed my entire life was about to happen. I was driving back from the Bendigo Court when I heard on the car radio that Anthony Farrell had been arrested in connection with the Walsh Street murders.

Not long afterwards, on one of the earliest mobile phones – which was the size of a house brick and weighed about as much – Charlie Nikakis rang me and told me the same thing. He said that he had been to the watch house for a quick discussion with Farrell but that I should go because of my long-standing association with Farrell's family, particularly his dad, Anthony senior. Farrell had already been in court and had protested his innocence in open court by screaming out that Jason Ryan was a "fucking liar and it was all bullshit". In addition, I was told by Charlie that Farrell had denied any knowledge or participation in the murders when he had spoken to him.

As a suspect in any crime, one is not required to answer any questions or make any admissions against one's own interest. That is, you are not obliged to confess to anything.

As a criminal lawyer, one's obligation is to advise one's client of their rights and suggest as forcibly as possible that they keep his mouth shut and say nothing that might come back to bite them later. I always gave that advice. I rarely advised clients to talk to the police because you never knew what might bob up down the track that could be beneficial to your defence if you have said nothing.

In this vein, I arrived at the City Watch House the next morning to see Anthony Farrell. I kept a transcript of our conversation, which – I should warn – is full of swearing. I have been criticised for it roundly over the years. Unfortunately, it was replayed in its entirety on national radio and TV, notwithstanding the fact that it was a privileged conversation between solicitor and client and was never meant to be for public consumption. Remember, I was talking to a kid with no education who had been brought up in Port Melbourne and was, at the time of his arrest, living in a car. Often the only way to communicate with such people is to talk on their wavelength, even if that style of language might normally be abhorrent to you – years of experience had taught me that. I must admit that I was also excited at being given instructions in this case as it was the biggest thing going in the criminal law at the time.

Fraser: Anthony how are ya mate?

Farrell: Not bad.

Fraser: Bit of a silly question isn't it?

Farrell: Yeah.

Fraser: Mate, you've said nothing have you?

Farrell: No, just told them where I was when.

Fraser: That's good, alright then. I reckon the way to do it … Charlie (Nikakis) and I have had a yarn about it. It is just whacking in an application into the Supreme Court fucking straight away. Because these cunts have got nothing on you.

Farrell: Yeah, I know. I know that Andrew.

Fraser: Yeah, well, they've got nothing on you so if we whomp a Supreme Court file application fucking straight in, we'll flush the cunts out.

Farrell: Yeah.

Fraser: They'll have to come up with it and they've got no fucking evidence.

Farrell: Yeah because Jason … Apparently they said …

Fraser: I don't give a fuck what they said about Jason either because if Jason's turned fuckin' dog …

Farrell: Yeah, that's right. Victor would have been pinched by now.

Fraser: Shhhh.

Farrell: Alright, we won't talk here, alright?

Fraser: I'm just here to let you know we're working on it. Not just Charlie, because I know your dad wants me in on it too, because I've known the family for a long while and while we are going to get you the best, mate, we're going to blow these cunts out of the water on this.

Farrell: I hope so.

Fraser: All you've got to do is fuckin keep your trap shut.

That means you're in custody now – you don't have to talk to any police. You understand that?

Farrell: Yeah.

Fraser: So say fucking nothing and don't consent to anything.

Farrell: I haven't.

Fraser: If they come into your cell, they'll be wired up.

Farrell: Oh yeah, I know that.

Fraser: So just keep your trap shut, mate. This is the rest of your life here because, don't worry, if you go down on this, you're going to get a fucking monster and we all know that, right?

Farrell: What? Never be released?

Fraser: I reckon that would just about be it, wouldn't it? It would have to be, wouldn't it?

Farrell: Mmm.

Fraser: Just keep calm son, alright. We've put the word out that you have said nothing because they were concerned you might have said something.

Farrell: I don't know nothing.

Fraser: I know that, but you know what jail talk is like.

Farrell: Yeah.

Fraser: Leave it to us. We'll have you up for bail in a couple of weeks' time alright. Vincent is coming in …

Farrell: Who is Vincent?

Fraser: Justice Vincent in the Supreme Court for bail, probably … about the best judge you could get.

Farrell: Yeah?

Fraser: We'll get you about the best fuckin' barristers around, mate, and we'll be there, alright?

Farrell: You reckon you could buy me a packet of smokes, Andrew?

Fraser: Yeah, sure, no problem.

Farrell: Hey, do I have to stay in my cell? – because they won't let me out.

Fraser: Yeah it's for your own fucking protection, mate. Now, what do you smoke – anything?

Farrell: Viscount. No, get me a packet of Peter Jacksons 30s.

Fraser: Right-oh. OK. Alright. So that's all I wanted to let you know, that we are working on it.

Farrell: Yeah, but when am I going to Pentridge?

Fraser: When there's room there.

Farrell: So I could have to stay in that cell for a month?

Fraser: Well, you could be there for a couple of weeks.

Farrell: What? In the cell?

Fraser: Yeah. Well, they've got to let you out for exercise, but only when there are no other blokes there.

Farrell: They haven't even been doing that.

Fraser: Yeah I know that mate. They're concerned about your safety, right?

Farrell: Yeah.

Fraser: So just leave all that to us. If it means you've got to put up with it, you've got to put up with it, right?

Farrell: Yeah.

Fraser: If you stop and think about it, it's about the worst murder that's ever been committed in this State and you're fucking IT for the time being. Now, what we've got to do is blow their case out of the fucking water, right? I'll tell you what they've done.

Farrell: Yeah.

Fraser: They've fucking nailed you because they reckon you're the weak link in the chain. They're putting fucking enormous pressure on you in what they are doing. They want you to be the one that cracks and gives everybody up. We're stronger than that.

Farrell: Yeah, I know that.

Fraser: So if you sit there and be strong, we'll get you out of it, alright? I'll get you some smokes, mate. I've got to fly but I just wanted to drop in and let you know that we are all in the rort for you.

Farrell: Alright, how long do you reckon till I go to the Supreme Court?

Fraser: A couple of weeks, mate.

Farrell: A couple of weeks?

Fraser: Well, it takes 10 days at the best of times, mate. It will be the week after next because Vincent is on and we want Vincent, alright?

Farrell: Yeah

Fraser: He's the man we want. OK?

Farrell: Alright.

Fraser: Good on ya, mate.

Farrell: Thanks a lot.

Fraser: No worries.

And with that I left the City Watch House at Russell Street.

Little did I know that entire conversation had been taped by the police in their first ever taping of a solicitor talking to his client in the cells at Russell Street – or in any cells in the state of Victoria, for that matter.

Now, while I concede that I probably over-egged the pudding in relation to the swearing in that discussion I had with Farrell, the advice I gave him was still valid: first, that he needed to assure me he had said nothing; second, keep your mouth shut from now on because the coppers will be wired up and try every trick in the book to get you to make admissions that you aren't required at law to make.

Regardless of the legitimacy or otherwise of that advice, it has come back to haunt me ever since 1988 – and that is some twenty years ago. I don't know how many times over the years police who I don't even know have either abused me on the telephone or at court, or refused to talk to me at all, because I was the bloke who gave Farrell "that" advice on Walsh Street. They were all dirty on me because the advice I gave was correct and Farrell followed my advice and said nothing else to anybody. He declined to be further interviewed and continued to deny any involvement, protesting his innocence at every opportunity.

What we didn't know at the time of the taping was that the police had put a great deal of store in the fact that they had Farrell and my assessment was correct: they thought he was weak and would be the one to tumble and give everybody up. That is assuming he knew anything about the case, which he, to this day, says he didn't.

For me what this did was suddenly place me right in the frame as far as the coppers were concerned. They were absolutely screaming mad that I'd given this advice and that Farrell was following it. He was their big ace and now it looked like they were not going to be able to play it. What followed was extraordinary behaviour by the police towards a solicitor giving proper professional advice.

First off, a detective by the name of Erol Mustufa came to my house one night for a beer and, while sitting in my house, said to me that Noonan (John Noonan, who was in charge of the Ty-Eyre Task Force) knew that I knew where the firearm was that had killed Tynan and Eyre and that if I didn't tell them, I would be arrested. I knew Mustafa through our shared athletics club and as a result had socialised with him on the odd occasion. The police used this as a lever for Mustafa to try to tumble me. To say that I was dumbfounded is an understatement. Here was a bloke who was supposed to be a friend, notwithstanding the fact that he is a copper, in my house, drinking my beer and threatening me. I couldn't believe my ears. I said, "I don't know what you are talking about, Erol, but it's time you left" and I threw him out.

From that moment, Mustafa and I ceased to be friends. How dare he come into my house and threaten me when he knew nothing about the case at all and had merely been used as a conduit by other coppers to try to rattle me! Well, it worked. I was completely thrown by this, but nowhere near as much as a couple of weeks later when a Detective Sergeant Colin McLaren from the Ty-Ayre task force contacted me at work and had a discussion with me along the lines that John Noonan has asked him to talk to me. "I want to meet you and have a discussion with you," he said. "The meeting will be on Saturday at the Shrine of Remembrance", which is in the Domain in Melbourne. McLaren told me that I was to turn up in runners (no socks), shorts and a singlet – nothing else. He would be wearing the same to make sure we both weren't wired.

I turned up at 1.00 pm on the Saturday. My heart was in my mouth. I didn't know what was going to happen to me on this day. I fully expected that I would either be bashed or killed by the police because of the way they had been behaving generally around Melbourne at that time.

When I got out of my car, I saw that McLaren was already there and he was alone. He frisked me and made me take my singlet off. I got him to do the same. He said, "Let's walk this way", indicating towards Punt Road. I said "No" and walked off in the other direction down towards the Shrine. I was not walking into a trap.

Our meeting lasted for about an hour, during which time

McLaren challenged me that I knew where the gun was that had been used to kill the two police, which was utter crap. I didn't even know what sort of a gun had been used at that stage, let alone where it was. They said they had an inkling of where the firearm was but couldn't find it and I knew, and that if I didn't tell them I would be arrested.

At the end of the conversation I was nearly sick with anxiety. I feared that I was going to be loaded up (that is, fabricated evidence planted on me). I can remember, as clear as if it were yesterday, talking to McLaren at the end of the discussion and hearing him say "You have seven days to produce the firearm." I said to him, "Colin, you know I don't know where the firearm is." "You know that what you've put to me is a lie. If you arrest me, yes, I will have trouble getting bail because it's in relation to a police murder. But believe me, you will not fuck my life. I know that you have been in the police force a long while and you will have a big superannuation fund." He conceded that. I then added "If you try to fuck my life, trust me I will fuck yours. If it's the last thing I do, I will sue you until I get every last penny of not only your superannuation but Noonan's as well and I'll sue the Victorian Government into the bargain for your behaviour. If it is the last thing I do, I will make sure you die in penury." That conversation is burnt into my memory as if it were yesterday.

I then went back to my home. As I walked in the front door my wife said, "What in god's name has happened to you?" She said I looked dreadful. I told her what had happened. She was completely dumbfounded by it as well. There was never another word from the police about me knowing where the firearm was.

It emerged that my discussion with Farrell had effectively torpedoed the entire prosecution case and when this matter went to court there was really no evidence on which a reasonable jury could convict.

If ever there had been trial by media, this case was it. If you believed what the media had written about this case, it would have been abundantly clear that four of the accused, namely Peirce, McEvoy, Pettingill and Farrell, were guilty of these offences. The jury and the trial judge (who, coincidentally, happened to be His Honour, Mr Justice Vincent) were the only ones who heard the evidence in its entirety and at the conclusion of the trial returned a verdict of "not guilty". That was the end of the case as far as those four accused were concerned. But it certainly wasn't the end of the line for others.

It had always been alleged that Jed Houghton was one of the killers. Houghton was on the run and was in a caravan park in Bendigo when the Special Operations Group – SOG (or, as they call themselves, "Sons of God") – knocked on the door of the caravan. The stories are varied here. The official line is that Houghton produced a firearm and pointed it at police, whereupon Houghton was shot in the chest and in the arm, dying instantly. Others say it was a summary execution by the coppers to get rid of a person who had murdered a police officer in their line of duty but on whom they had insufficient evidence.

One Gary Abdullah was alleged to have obtained the motor vehicle for the Walsh Street murders. Abdullah was found in his flat in Carlton by detectives Cliff Lockwood and Dermot Avon on 6 December 1988. Abdullah was shot seven times by Cliff Lockwood – six times by Lockwood with his own service revolver which he emptied into him, then once more with Avon's firearm. Lockwood's defence at his subsequent murder trial was that the shooting was accidental. The jury accepted his defence and Lockwood was acquitted of murder. One must wonder, though, how you can shoot somebody accidentally seven times, particularly when you are required to change firearms to do so. However, the jury's verdict is final and Cliffy gets the benefit of the doubt.

Even though this matter is now nineteen years old, certain questions over Walsh Street still remain unanswered and will probably never go away. Victor Peirce's wife Wendy was in witness protection for a very long period of time between the murders and the trial getting on. During that time Wendy had indicated that she was going to give Crown evidence against Victor, which would have effectively sunk everybody. The trial came and went. Wendy gave evidence but somersaulted the police and said that Victor had nothing to do with the shooting of Tynan and Eyre. That was another severe blow. That wasn't the end of the matter, though. Only about twelve months ago, Wendy came out and stated in the media she had lied about Victor to protect him and that Victor Peirce was one of the shooters at Walsh Street. This was all academic by then because Victor Peirce had been killed earlier in a drug-related murder by persons unknown.

The theory still persists that it was the death of Graeme Jensen that brought about the payback killing of two innocent police. The police have always maintained that Jensen had a firearm with him and pointed it at them, thus requiring them to shoot to protect themselves. Detective Sergeant Malcolm Rozenes, who has just concluded a jail sentence for corruption and drug trafficking, in an attempt to save himself, made many statements to police regarding corrupt police activity. One, which is probably the most startling, was the allegation made by Rozenes that he was at the scene at Narre Warren when Jensen was shot and that he gave the sawn off .22 rifle to the members of the Armed Robbery Squad to throw into Jensen's car after they had, in effect, executed him. That allegation seems to have gone nowhere and it remains unanswered. With Wendy Pierce's allegations and Rozenes' allegations, it appears that the matter of Walsh Street will not go away and will hang around for a very long time to come. Its impact on me was profound. Ultimately, though, no one was hurt as much as the families of Steven Tynan and Damian Eyre. My heart goes out to them because, irrespective of who did what, two young policemen did not deserve to be executed in the manner in which they were merely because they were wearing a blue uniform.

After the trial and acquittal, I learned that Derryn Hinch, a Melbourne news reporter and current affairs host, was going to run the entirety of the tape of my discussion with Farrell in the city watch house on his evening show. I took out an injunction in the Supreme Court of Victoria to try to stop the playing of that tape on the basis that it was professionally privileged and in any event I didn't particularly want the fruity language I had used made a matter of public record.

The matter proceeded before His Honour Mr Justice O'Bryan, who was less than impressed with my swearing. Typical: more interested in the form than the substance, even though (or because?) the substance was correct. If I was still a criminal lawyer and if I were advised to give anybody in Farrell's position advice again, I would unhesitatingly give the same advice. It was the correct advice and if he had been forced into making admissions, whether those admissions were true or false, he would never have been released from jail. I lost the injunction application and Hinch played the entire discussion on his TV show that night.

In about 1991 or so I began to become disillusioned with my then practice. I was working excessively long hours and, frankly, supplementing the financial returns to other partners (with one exception) as I was far and away the greatest generator of work and income. I felt I was being used and was stuck in a rut.

It is funny how things work out – not always for the best, as my next move shows – but it felt right at the time. It transpired that another firm, Galbally & Rolfe, were not travelling all that well and needed a new infusion of work. They didn't mind how they got the work, only that they got their hands on it. I was the conduit to their new work and the long and short of it is that I was head-hunted to the new firm of Galbally Fraser & Rolfe. My income rocketed and the first exclusively criminal defence firm was the talk of the town. I had landed Alan Bond as a client just before departing Haines Blakie and Polites and the future looked rosy indeed.

The building magnate Bruno Grollo was about to be charged with perverting the course of justice, a charge he later was acquitted of, and Rolfe was instructed to act for Bruno's right-hand man, Bob Howard. Two cases the size of Bond and Grollo kicked the firm off with a bang.

I still wanted to maintain my everyday base of clients because, while the big cases were going, all was fine, but all cases finish and I realised we needed to maintain our broad base for the future. My new partners, Brian Rolfe and Bob Galbally, disagreed, saying I should do nothing but Bond and the other white-collar cases I was advising on at the time.

My attitude to practice building was, and had always been, to use my grandfather's saying "A sprat to catch a mackerel". In other words, it was often good business to risk a small amount in order to establish goodwill and thereby generate more lucrative work further down the track. I was always prepared to punt being paid for a bail application in order to be instructed for the trial. Often blokes you had punted on being paid by not only came good with their cash but also tipped in their mates who found themselves in bother with the wallopers. This is how I managed to generate such a large practice.

The mindset of my new partners flew in the face of this attitude. "No dough, no defence" was the mantra. It was distressing to me, as soon the old punters drifted elsewhere.

On reflection I should not have allowed myself to be seduced by Brian and Bob into the new firm but my income doubled overnight and the new offices were terrific. Doing all the high-flying cases, I was starting to believe my own bullshit!

During the first few years with GF&R we could not put a foot wrong. In addition to Bond and Grollo, which both went on for years, I acted for the footballer Jimmy Krakouer when he appealed against his sentence and conviction for trafficking a commercial quantity of methyl amphetamine in Western Australia. The appeal proceeded all the way to the High Court and we won, with a retrial being ordered.

I travelled to Perth to make a bail application for Jimmy pending his retrial, and the application was successful. As we all know, football is popular in this country but I was staggered at the media coverage of Jimmy's case. As we left the court I knew there was media waiting for us but what greeted us surprised even me. There were more cameras for Jimmy Krakouer the footballer than for Americas Cup winner Alan Bond!

Unfortunately Legal Aid took over Jimmy's retrial and he was convicted and sentenced to a huge term of imprisonment. Jimmy is now, like me, on parole. I hope all is well for him.

The Bond and Grollo cases inevitably drew to their respective conclusions, Grollo being acquitted and Bondy heading off to the slammer for a holiday. We were faced with the prospect of doing the local court rounds again, which did not faze me at all as I enjoyed the cut and thrust of criminal law at the coal face. Brian, in particular, was not at all keen on this and, at the same time my use was increasing. All these ingredients did not make for a particularly pleasant working environment.

So ended a brief five-year period in another partnership, but a spectacular one. I had hit the highest notes possible for a solicitor but little did I know that now I was about to plumb the lowest depths, beyond my wildest imagination.

In retrospect the worst thing that could have happened at that time was for me not to have the discipline that attaches to a partnership and the obligation to others that that carries with it. I was now a one man band accountable to nobody. I could get off my face if I wanted to – with, I thought, impunity. How wrong I was.

I was already struggling with the demon that is a cocaine addiction and now that I was a sole practitioner things started to go seriously wrong. I clearly recall being in the bathroom one morning before work and seeing myself in the mirror. "Fraser," I said to myself, "you have a cocaine addiction and your life will go down the toilet unless you pull up. You will not use today." Needless to say, that good intention lasted until I left court and I got into it again.

When you are addicted, you have no control over your usage and the climate in the legal profession was such that I felt I had no one I could confide in and seek help. My wife was at her wits' end: nothing she said could make me change my ways. I had a one-way ticket to oblivion.

As I have said, criminal law is like living in a pressure cooker. Consider this, when you head off to court in the morning you are not exactly off to a flying start. Your client usually thinks he has paid you too much to begin with. You are opposed to coppers who generally don't like you or the punter. The prosecutor thinks you are shifty (the compliment is usually reciprocated) and the judge is grumpy because he or she doesn't like their job. It doesn't exactly add up to a very cheerful existence.

I have seen a lot of innocent blokes "fitted up" by the coppers and go to jail when they shouldn't. This hurts. Worse still is the bloke you think is as hot as a spud and he walks, insufficient evidence. None of these things enhance confidence in the system and it gradually gets you down. You try and leave it all behind in the office but it is the nature of the beast that you carry it with you all the time. The degree of cynicism and callousness you develop is amazing.

As a consequence blokes hit the bottle, play up on their spouses or – as in my case – hop into drugs, and despite the self-serving mutterings to the contrary there are plenty who do drugs. Some pinch their trust accounts and blow the lot on the punt. When they are inevitably caught they also end up in the nick.

You are always watching your back against dissatisfied clients, although I must say I was fortunate in that I was never threatened by a client over a bad result. Lots of lawyers were and it would not be a pleasant experience.

My practice, notwithstanding my problems, started to rebuild once word filtered out. Many of my old clients returned to me, stating they had left in the interim because they did not like my former partners. But it didn't matter now how well my business was going because the end was nigh. I had been on my own for just on a year and, as a result of my close relationship with Werner Roberts, things had spiralled seriously out of control. I was not only using on a daily basis, I was using a lot.

The week before my arrest I travelled to Perth to appear for Pasquale ("Little Pat") Barbaro, who was later murdered with Jason Moran at a kids' footy clinic in Essendon. Barbaro had been charged with trafficking a large amount of methyl amphetamine by taking it from Melbourne to Perth. He pleaded guilty and received a very light sentence. A great result, notwithstanding my condition. The point of this story is twofold: first, I was still able to keep it together long enough each day to function to a reasonably normal degree in court. Secondly: The night before I appeared I was in my hotel and

I had a premonition that the wheels were about to fall off my life and I could see no end to it all. The next morning, while walking along St Georges Terrace, I contemplated suiciding, leaving my wife with the proceeds of my life insurance policies. She would be better off without me.

I did not have the guts to throw myself under the buses that hurtle along that road and I have lived to tell my tale. I hope that someone reading may take heed and gain strength from what befell me. The journey is difficult but well worth the effort.

The following weekend I was arrested and charged. My life had changed forever but now I have developed sufficient insight to realise that everything that happens in your life happens for a reason. Fortunately the reason was a positive and I have been fortunate enough to have another go at life. If I had not been pulled up so abruptly, I now realise I would have probably died from drug use.

Chapter 7
In the Slammer

I'm hiding in Honduras
And I'm a desperate man.
Send lawyers, guns and money,
The shit has hit the fan.

LAWYERS, GUNS AND MONEY, WARREN ZEVON

Jail is a desolate place. I had been sentenced to a minimum of five years' imprisonment and this was a period of time that, from where I was now sitting, had no end in sight. The futility that stretches out in front of you under such circumstances is almost overwhelming. I did my best to try to get my head around what had happened to me, but it was clear that the only way to deal with my fate was not to think about the entirety of the sentence but rather to deal with each day as it came. I could not afford to think any further ahead than the next day. To use the old expression, you just "put one foot in front of the other". If you look after the days, the months will eventually look after themselves and in due course the years will go by.

I tried to get myself into a routine and fill my days as best I could. Fortunately I had always been an avid reader, and I started reading again. I had as many books as possible sent in to me because I had approximately six or eight hours' reading time per day to fill.

Even such a simple request as a book met with extraordinary institutional resistance. At MAP, where I was first placed, as I have said I was not allowed to have books with hard covers. My mother brought in a book for me to read, Bryce Courtenay's then new novel Four Fires, and the officer in charge promptly told her I couldn't have it because it had a hard cover. A woman to be reckoned with, my mother immediately tore the cover off the book and gave the insides to the officer. I subsequently received the book, read it and enjoyed it. Once I got to Port Phillip, however, with each and every book that somebody sent me I had to list its title, its author and whether it had a hard cover – and then some clown would make an arbitrary decision as to whether I could have the book. When you have somebody who can barely read, let alone read the contents of a book, their authority to make decisions on what you may or may not read is not an easy thing to accept. Also, a mate of mine made sure the newspapers were delivered to me each day and that kept me in touch with the outside world.

Mind you, the vetting of books was something the screws were rarely required to do, given the literacy level of the average prisoner, so from the word go I was singled out for special treatment. The screws seemed to be somewhat intimidated by the fact that I was educated and a former lawyer. This also gave them a reason to try and stand over me, getting even in some perverse way. I soon learned what was required of me and gained some idea of my rights, so I stuck to my guns and would not swear, scream at, or abuse them. My attitude was that if I had a question, they were obliged to answer. This often showed the screws up because they either did not know the answer or could not be bothered answering. My persistence became a sticking point to the degree that there is a mention of it in my prison file and in reports on me to which I have had access. Singled out because I stuck up for myself and often helped others who had no idea.

The jail routine was monotonous and, as I have said, the highlight of each day was gym from 10 till 11 each morning. That gave you access to weights machines or the use of the small running track that I have referred to. I decided to use my time outside to get fresh air and I walked and walked. Then, as I got stronger, I started to jog again and at the end of each hour I would try a few minutes' weights. Once I returned to my cell I would continue with push-ups and sit-ups regularly throughout the day.

One day in the gym I heard over the loud speaker: "Fraser, Sentence Management." I said to the screw, "Where is

Sentence Management?" He said, "Back in the unit. We will take you up there now."

I had been waiting some months to see Sentence Management. This was February 2002 and I had been in custody since November 2001.

If one goes to the website for the Victorian Department of Justice it states that Sentence Management is designed to discuss and work with the prisoner for the purposes of setting out an appropriate regime for the serving of the prisoner's sentence and to assist with his rehabilitation.

I was taken back to my cell, where I put my gym stuff, and was then taken to Sentence Management. I walked in the door and sitting there was a man called Ron Orr. The conversation went like this:

Fraser: Good Morning

Orr: You're a fucking pest aren't you?

Fraser: I beg your pardon.

Orr: You heard me. You're a fucking pest.

Fraser: Why?

Orr: You are going to Port Phillip – Sirius East – and that's the end of the story.

Fraser: Hold on a minute, I thought Sentence Management was for me to discuss my placement with you.

Orr: You are not listening to me. You are going to Sirius East at Port Phillip.

Fraser: I want to go to Loddon [a country jail near Castlemaine] where I can pursue my education.

Orr: You are going to Port Phillip.

Fraser: When am I going?

Orr: Now.

Fraser: What do you mean, now?

Orr: I said now. Go and pack your cell, you are being moved before lunch.

Fraser: Can I ring my family?

Orr: No, the phone has been disconnected. You are not allowed to tell anybody about your movement for security reasons.

Fraser: How am I going to be able to tell my wife where I am?

Orr: I don't give a fuck. Get moving.

That was the entirety of the discussion I had with Mr Orr about my placement, my rehabilitation and my further education. What a terrific institution Sentence Management is, and there's more about that later.

After that abrupt meeting I was immediately marched back to my cell and I was not allowed to shower, even though I had been in the gym for almost an hour. The screws stood there while I packed my cell. My head was spinning and I had my heart in my mouth. What is going on here? Why am I being sent to Sirius East at Port Phillip? I don't even know anything about Port Phillip. Why am I being sent to "protection from protection" in a maximum security prison when I am not a risk to anybody? None of these questions have ever been answered for me and each time I have asked, the questions have either been ignored or greeted with the inevitable jail response: "Get fucked. If you don't like what's happened to you, don't come to jail."

After I packed my cell I was marched downstairs and, much to my surprise, I was greeted by two giants of men who were prison officers but not from MAP. They were from Barwon Prison, which is down near Geelong, outside Melbourne, and their sole job is to move prisoners who are a risk. These men were enormous and were in no mood for any backchat.

Even though the screws had been present while I packed my cell, all my stuff was immediately upended and searched again. I was then strip-searched again and, much to my surprise and disgust, a set of shackles and leg irons was produced and the biggest screw said "Put these on." I said, "You have got to be joking. What in God's name am I being shackled for?" He said, "If you don't put the fucking things on, we'll hold you down and put them on for you."

Try imagining being leg-ironed and shackled. The paraphernalia that I was placed in was a large belt something like a weightlifter's belt, with a big steel ring at the front through which hand cuffs are passed, you are then handcuffed to that belt, meaning you cannot move your hands more than a few inches. Also attached to that steel ring is a chain that runs down to your ankles and there is a T-piece at the bottom of that chain with two short chains (and I mean short) which go to each ankle. There the leg irons are then locked onto you at your ankles. So there I was standing with my hands cuffed at my sides and in leg irons. What depths had I plummeted to?

The chains were so short that I could not walk properly. The best I could do was a quick hobble. I was filthy about being trussed up like a Christmas turkey and I said, "Why is this being done?" The screw said, "You are a risk." I said, "Well, that is utter bullshit. Am I at risk or am I the risk? To which the screw said, "You are at risk." I said, "Well, that makes abundant sense, shackling me and leg-ironing me so that if somebody jumps me between here and the van, I've got no hope at all of protecting myself." The screw merely looked at me and shrugged.

Then, still in leg irons and in handcuffs, I was placed in a holding cell where I was left for a couple of hours. I don't know why, but I was then marched out of the cell and to a van on my own. I was placed in the back of the van in a cage which was just big enough for my shoulders – and I am not a big man – and then the front of the cage was closed on me. No safety belt. (I wonder what the government thinks about that?) The cage door was closed so there I was sitting in a cage just big enough to take the width of my shoulders and with my knees hard up against the door of the cage. No safety belt. I was nearly beside myself with fear. The door was closed and the van was completely blacked out. I could not see my hand in front of my face.

As a lawyer I had been to Port Phillip on many, many occasions, so I had a rough idea of where we were going. I knew when we were heading up the Westgate Bridge and I had an idea from the movement of the van when we were going down the Westgate Bridge. I knew that, at about three or four kilometres before the jail, there was very large round-about and as we went around that roundabout I could feel it in the van and that was the only indication for me that I was nearing Port Phillip.

I've forgotten to mention that the leg irons were so short that I could not step into the van properly and I had to be lifted in and had to be turned around and plonked into the seat before the door was slammed on me. The van had clearly arrived at Port Phillip as I could hear voices and gates opening and closing.

The van came to a stop and the back door was opened. I found the sunshine nearly blinding after having spent I don't know how long locked in pitch darkness. I was lifted down from the van by the two screws, as I couldn't get out otherwise, only to be confronted by about twenty faces staring at me through the laundry workshop window, which was adjacent to where I was taken from the van. I was taken inside and the leg irons and shackles were removed. My head was spinning. I didn't know what to think.

Writing this book now, I am still deeply distressed at the thought of what happened to me. I was nearly vomiting with fear and apprehension. Once again I was strip-searched. What in God's name I was supposed to have obtained, handcuffed in a cage inside a van, I do not know. I said earlier there is nothing as demeaning as a strip search, and that is true, but the more you are subjected to them, the less they bother you. In the end it was a bit like changing your socks: you just wore it and got on with it.

I was taken inside and all my belongings (one basketful) were upended yet again and searched yet again. Absolutely nothing in there that I wasn't allowed to have, but a number of things were still taken from me. Books that I had brought with me from MAP were confiscated on the pretext that they had not been approved at Port Phillip. I had an argument with the authorities about that. "Too bad, you are not having these books, they have not been approved." It was at this stage that I decided I was going to have to be firm about some of my treatment by the screws and I was persistent but polite.

Never during my sentence did I yell, or swear, at a screw or abuse or threaten them. As it turned out, my policy of being politely persistent intimidated the screws far more than the other blokes standing around shouting the usual gratuitous abuse that they had heard probably thousands of times before in their careers.

The jail was locked down and everything had to be cleared while I was marched up to Sirius East. I can remember walking along carrying my pathetic basket of the few belongings that I was allowed to keep and, as I was walking along the area near the hospital, I looked around. Port Phillip is a privately run prison and is a maximum security facility. Boy, was I ever in jail now! All around were concrete, steel bars and razor wire. Nothing but desolation and futility filled my mind at that time. I said to myself, "Fraser, you have been in jail three months now. You have four years and nine months of this still to go. You haven't even started your sentence yet, and look where you have ended up already. Boy, have you landed yourself in the shit here, well and truly!"

I arrived at Sirius East, which is, as I said, protection from protection. It quickly became obvious that I had not been placed there for my own protection. The real reason I was placed in Sirius East was to take me away from the mainstream where I had a lot of former clients who would have made my time in jail a lot more comfortable. Instead, I was placed in with the worst of the worst. Some of my unit mates were Raymond Edmunds (Mr Stinky), who killed Garry Heywood and Abina Madill; the serial killer Peter Dupas; the Bega school girl murderer Leslie Camilleri; rapist Christopher Hall; and serial paedophile Andrew Davies.

As you can see, there is some disparity between the seriousness of my crime and their crimes. Once again, I was not told that I had to seek protection and sign a protection form. All I was told, when I was taken off the van, was that if I was going to "knock" myself (kill myself) that I shouldn't do that and if I felt like I was going to knock myself to let them know and the powers that be would make arrangements for me to have psychiatric treatment.

At Sirius East I was taken into the office of the supervisor, one Cyril Fox, a former South African Army officer, who revelled in his job of locking blokes up. I sat there with Mr Fox and another supervisor and was effectively read the riot act as to the behaviour required in the unit, etc., etc., etc., and the claim that I was there for my own protection. I wish I knew then what I know now about being in protection. At the time, I merely accepted that this must be the way it's done and therefore I was in protection for the remainder of my sentence.

I asked about education. I had been thinking that, if my appeal was unsuccessful, I would be able to complete at least one more degree before the end of my long sentence. No such luck, as things turned out.

After having the riot act read to me I asked when I could phone my wife. Fox said "Your phone credits have not been transferred from MAP as yet and accordingly the phone is not available." After some discussion, and in the presence of four officers (why four officers needed to be in the room while I was talking to my wife I do not know), I was allowed to make a phone call to my wife for two minutes to tell her that I had been moved and where I was. She was as shocked as I was.

My strongest memory of this meeting was how extraordinarily smug and superior the screws were. They knew full well who I was and they were going to make my life as difficult as they could by lording it over me for the entirety of my sentence. It gave me a feeling of foreboding – and that feeling turned out to be justified.

I was removed from the office and taken to my cell. It was a double cell and I was to share it with the serial paedophile

Andrew Davies. Davies, for his umpteenth offence of paedo-philia, received a life sentence with no minimum. However, on appeal that sentence was reduced and I understand he now has a minimum.

I am a father and at that time my children were young. You can imagine the revulsion I felt when I was placed in a cell with a person such as this. This man was about as low a scumbag as it is possible to imagine. He kept denying his crimes to me. He wanted me to read his brief, which I did, and I was revolted to the degree that I did not want to talk to him at all. Yet you have no option because you are banged up in a cell about three by two and a half metres for many hours per day, and you just have to get on with it.

I have never smoked cigarettes and this bloke was not only a chain smoker but, because he had no money, he spent his time going through the rubbish tins and retrieving other blokes' butts, which he would then reassemble into cigarettes and smoke these in the cell. Can you imagine the stench in the cell from those twice-smoked cigarettes? It was putrid and the ventilation in the cell was woefully wanting. Frankly, I doubt whether it complies with the minimum ventilation standard required by law.

The cell had two bunks in it and had clearly been designed by a genius. The cells had bars running horizontal across the windows. Not only were the bars horizontal, providing a per-fect hanging opportunity, but they were on the inside of the windows! Within a very short time after Port Phillip Prison was opened, somebody had hung himself from those bars. In jail nothing is proactive – everything is reactive. In other words, nobody thinks anything through in advance, but when something unforeseen happens, the furore that follows is spectacular and often highly amusing.

The reaction to the hanging in the brand-new jail was that those bars were covered by another sheet of high-tensile clear plastic, which removed the possibility of the bars being used as a hanging point. The only trouble with that was that the half of the window that you could open for ventilation was obstructed. Therefore two grown men were required to coexist in a cell less than half the size of a single garage with one window that was about 30 to 40 centimetres wide and about 15 centimetres high. I don't think that's sufficient ventilation. I have never suffered from claustrophobia but after a short time of being locked in these cells for extended periods I started to feel claustrophobic. It is an awful feeling and I think it was fuelled by the overwhelming sense of futility and hopelessness that I had at the time.

Lock-downs were a common occurrence and happened regularly. You would not be told why or when you were being locked down or the expected duration of the lock-down. It was something you merely had to endure. During each lock-down I was forced to sit for hours or days in my cell with absolutely nothing to do except read and endure idiotic ravings about Commodore cars, which were my cell mate's passion in life. My view of motor cars is that they are means of getting from A to B in a sitting position and, frankly, I couldn't care less about Commodores, let alone want to discuss them with him. It was during these times that my feelings of claustrophobia first manifested themselves. The cell I was placed in was down stairs facing west and it was high summer in Melbourne. This cell was as hot as an oven; add to that the smoking, the appalling ventilation and the fact that I was on the top bunk because I was the newest inmate in the cell, and it is no wonder that I started to suffer claustrophobia.

The first night came and went. I spent the long hours lying awake on the top bunk looking out of the window into no–man's land at the wall. Rabbits scurried under the wall through small drains and as I watched them come and go I pondered how long it would be before I was on the other side of that wall and whether I would make it.

One day one of the officers was bragging to me about how no one had ever escaped from Port Phillip and how it was escape proof. I pointed out to him that I bet I could walk straight out the front door without anybody realising. His reply was that such a suggestion was utter bullshit.

When you visit Port Phillip as a lawyer, you have a pin number, you have a reference number and you have a hand scan, all of which you need to go into and out of the prison. It was my bet that neither my hand scan nor my pin number had been removed from the system when I became an inmate. I shared this thought with the officer, who said he thought that was utter crap but he would check. He came back a while later with a big smirk on his face and said, "You were right. Your hand scan and pin number were still on the system as a professional visitor." If I had been able to get hold of a suit (which was not impossible), I would probably have been able to walk out the door using my old pin and hand scan. So much for Port Phillip being escape proof! Obviously they didn't bargain on having a solicitor as an inmate.

One of the foremost aspects of sentencing somebody is rehabilitation. Without exception every case you read that talks about sentencing people talks about rehabilitation. Unfortunately the high moral ground that the courts look to impose – namely, that all those who go to jail are rehabilitated – could not be further from the truth. The bottom line is that there is no rehabilitation in jail. The screws don't care. Sentence Management doesn't care and the people employed in the jail (that is, non prison officers) don't care either. The entire existence of a prison officer is dedicated to counting crooks on muster four times a day, watching television, being fed by crooks, smoking cigarettes, drinking coffee and generally doing as little as is humanly possible.

There was one officer who, if you went and asked him a question, would stand up, grab his crotch, wiggle his hand up and down and say "suck my big fat one". What a terrific, professional approach to adopt to a sensible question being asked of you.

At Port Phillip prisoners were theoretically allowed eleven hours a day out of their cells. As soon as I was let out of my cell on the first day I decided to try to get a job and I was told that I could start on "nuts and bolts" tomorrow. "Nuts and bolts" at Port Phillip is just that. In other words, as a lawyer of twenty-eight years' standing at that time, my rehabilitation consisted of assembling what are known as Dyna bolts. Big bins of bolts, sleeves and nuts were delivered to the unit so that prisoners on nuts and bolts could sit at a table in the workroom and assemble them. You took a bolt, you placed the sleeve on it and then you put a nut on the bolt, and you did this for five hours a day. Fantastic rehabilitation! Of course, my vast experience in the assembly of nuts and bolts has been of invaluable assistance to me since my release!

There was one interesting thing about the layout of Sirius East. As you walked into the unit, there was an officers' station, which was slightly elevated. This gave the officers an uninterrupted view of both downstairs and the first tier of the unit. You then walked to the other end of the unit, out into what we called the "chook pen", which was a small exercise yard that we could use whenever we were out of our cells. The chook pen was the width of the unit – on my estimation, about 12 metres. It was about 5 metres deep. On the other side of the chook pen was the workroom. This room had no windows, so it was impossible for the screws to see in. There were a couple of benches, a toilet and a sink where we could make a brew (coffee or tea). Brews are an important part of jail. Everybody is obsessed with constantly drinking jail coffee (coffee, milk and two sugars). I was an exception: I drank mostly water because I found the coffee undrinkable.

Not only was the workroom not visible from the officers' station but it was also not supervised from within. A supervisor might wander down and have a look into the room once a day if we were lucky. So essentially we were all left to our own devices. It was out here that the jail shivs (knives or stabbing implements) were manufactured. Somebody could sit on the floor and use the concrete to sharpen the knives while others kept a lookout and if a screw started to walk in our direction a signal would be given and the sharpening would cease.

On another occasion a young bloke who had constantly resisted the sexual advances of another prisoner was raped. He was taken into the toilet and bashed, then his anus was slit with a razor blade and he passed out. He regained consciousness only to find himself bent over the toilet being raped from behind. Imagine the impact that has had on that young man's life. He has now lost his reason and his drug use has gone through the roof.

I stuck with the nuts and bolts for as long as I possibly could but the prospect of other jobs was dim. I noticed that the notorious Peter Dupas was the gardener and an Asian prisoner who didn't have the faintest idea about gardening was his assistant. I asked about the possibility of becoming a gardener and was told that I would have to wait for one of the two current gardeners to either lose their job or move to another jail. So nuts and bolts it was for time being.

When we weren't working, I sat in my cell and kept very

much to myself, for the very simple reason that I wasn't the least bit interested in mixing with any of these people and I was still trying to come to terms with what had befallen me.

One morning I was walking up and down in the chook pen with a bloke called Paul Gorman, who was in for a number of rapes and freely admitted that he would offend again (and he had at that stage served over ten years for rape). He told me that the only way I would be able to cope with my incarceration was to not let my mind go out over the wall but rather to dedicate my entire focus to being incarcerated and let the wall encapsulate my whole existence. In other words, there was no such thing as the outside world. I looked at this bloke, thought about how long he had done and looked at his complete lack of rehabilitation. I then came to the conclusion that the only way to properly deal with my sentence was to resolve that the authorities may well have my body but they would not have my mind. My mind would never be inside the jail. I would dedicate myself to keeping in touch with what was going on in the outside world and my entire mental existence would be outside the wall. In other words, the exact opposite of what Gorman had recommended. That turned out to be the right decision as the comings and goings of the outside world were the only thing that kept me sane during the indeterminably long days and nights that followed.

There was the occasional light moment, however. One day I was writing a letter to a friend and I wrote the word preposterous. Sometimes you write a word and even though you spell it correctly it just does not look right. So I was sitting there with the dictionary, looking up "preposterous". The unit clown, a bloke called Sonny, stuck his head in and said, "What are you looking up?" I said "preposterous". This is the truth: he said to me, "What is a preposterous?" I don't know what made me think of it but, quick as a flash, I said to him, "It's like a small rhinoceros", to which he replied, "Thanks very much", and off he trotted as happy as Larry.

I asked about further education and was told I had to apply. I asked to see the lady from education and when she arrived I informed her that I wished to do another degree. I didn't really care what that degree was, I said, as long as I was able to something worthwhile with my time. She said, "You have to apply for full-time education" and informed me she would bring the forms the next time she was at the jail. That never happened, despite my constantly requesting the forms. I was then told that I had to apply to be assessed as suitable for full-time education. Have you ever heard such crap in your life? I had been a practising lawyer for nearly thirty years and I had to justify to some jail clown that I had suitable intellect to be educated. Nevertheless, I kept up my requests and two years later – yes, two years later – a bloke from the education section turned up at the unit and said, "I am here to assess you for your suitability for full-time education." I could not believe my ears. Two years it had taken for this bloke to merely come and assess me as suitable or otherwise! I was furious. I sat down with him and said, "Before we go anywhere, I'd like you to tell me what qualifications you have that enable you to adequately assess my suitability for full-time education." I said, "I'm a practising lawyer, you know that. Do you have similar qualifications?" The silence was deafening. He pulled out the education assessment form and signed it blank, then gave it to me before leaving the room without another word. No full-time education for me, it transpired. Thank you very much to all the powers that be at Port Phillip and a big thank you, in particular, to the Corrections Commissioner, Mr Kelvin Anderson, for the wonderful way he administers the prison system under his watch.

As backup, I had also been writing to education facilities seeking to do another degree. Monash and Melbourne universities and Charles Sturt University in South Australia all didn't bother to reply to my letters. I wrote to Charles Sturt University three years in a row trying to enrol in a wine marketing course. To this day I have not had the courtesy of a reply from that university.

The only university that wrote back to me was the University of New England in Armidale, northern New South Wales. By the time I received the letter I had been moved to Fulham Correctional Centre near West Sale and I had then run out of time to complete any further qualifications, so I didn't bother. I had decided I would continue with my own education in British and Australian history and English literature, and to that end I read every book I could get my hands on.

When sentenced I was computer illiterate, so I decided I would try to enrol in a computer course. Port Phillip had a small computer room containing about ten computers – no more – to cater for a jail of some seven hundred blokes. That's not a terrific percentage and the chances of getting into the course were remote indeed. Once again, I kept asking and I was repeatedly told there were other blokes on the list in front of me.

I hope by now that the reader is getting some indication of the frustration I was feeling at the whole system and the way not only I in particular but all prisoners in general were treated when it comes to rehabilitation. You will hear all the self-justification and ass covering in the world from people like Mr Anderson but the fact is that nobody cares. There is no budget for rehabilitation and the unfortunate reality is that when blokes are released they are not rehabilitated. Now, society needs to come to terms with this fact. All that is happening at the moment is that prisoners are sentenced. They are effectively warehoused and segregated from the community for a given period of time. They are then released back into the community without having undergone any meaningful rehabilitation whatsoever. While in jail, people hone their criminal skills. There are constant discussions between crooks as to what new crimes they will commit. Any crime that is imaginable from murder to drug trafficking is planned to be executed when they leave jail. New criminal alliances and allegiances are formed and as they leave jail these allegiances and associations are continued on the outside. Jail is nothing more than a human warehouse and a university for advanced criminal learning.

With very few exceptions, everybody is going to be released from jail sooner or later. The question for the community at large is "Do we want people released with a better criminal repertoire than when they were incarcerated, or do we want people released from prison who are not using drugs, are not associating with criminals and are able to play a meaningful and productive role in society?" I would have thought the answer was blindingly obvious, but as there are no votes in jails, nothing is being done about it. Everybody from the Commissioner and Minister for Corrections to the judges in the courts will all say the exact opposite. I have seen the system with my own eyes. The system is broken, it doesn't work and we need to address some very hard questions but I know it will go no further because nobody has the political will or the guts to upend the whole system and start again.

At Port Phillip we had a period each day in which we were allowed into the garden area, which had a footpath around it that was 130 metres I length – a whole 50 metres more than at MAP. In addition to furthering my own education, I decided to embark on a strict regime of physical fitness. It was easy to lose weight in jail because you don't eat much of the food due to the fact that it is largely inedible. Port Phillip was where I also learnt the third and fourth lessons of jail, the third lesson being: don't drink the soup because the cooks piss in it and they think that is a huge joke; and the fourth, be careful of the food that you do eat.

One night rice custard was being served as dessert. The billet that was to serve the food took the lid off the stainless steel tray only to be greeted with the sight of a handful of pubic hair liberally sprinkled across the top of the rice custard. Yet another hilarious joke. But, believe it or not, some blokes just took the hairs off and ate the custard anyway!

As there were three units that used the same garden we were allowed between one and two hours a day in the garden of each unit. I started walking for the entire two hours and as my fitness improved I walked further. I walked and walked and walked. I preferred to walk on my own. I didn't want to talk to anybody. I wanted to be free to walk for two hours in the sunshine with my own thoughts, which were always outside the walls. As I got fitter, I walked further. I then started to jog and to do a few push-ups and a few sit-ups.

It was a long haul to get back to anywhere near the fitness that I had pursued my entire life. I had been a reasonably good athlete in my youth and had run the 400 metre hurdles at a pretty good level. I ran for Box Hill for many years when it was the strongest athletic club in Australia with outstanding athletes. The competition within the club for the top spots was intense. I loved the competition, even within the club, and on reflection it was character building for me. To be good required application and discipline. You cannot rely on anyone else; it is up to you entirely how you perform. I always enjoyed the challenge of training and racing. This application stood me in good stead to pursue my legal career, both by being fit and healthy and on the matter of application.

When I was jailed I was in a bad way, even though I was drug free by then. The stress and pressure had been unrelenting and now it was over – I was in the nick. What to do next to try and get my head right? I decided to get back into as much training as I was able. Training helped me in two ways: first, it helped fill in time and take my mind off where I was. Secondly, the exercise made me feel better and helped with my depression and particularly my panic attacks.

I can remember being out walking one day when I realised that I had been in jail a year. I was momentarily elated at the thought of one year down. I looked back at how long that year had taken. It seemed like ten years. I cannot begin to convey the feeling of frustration that each day brings because each day on the inside seems like a month on the outside. As I am writing this book I have been home nearly a year. I have no idea where that year has gone. It seems like yesterday that I was released, whereas a year in jail had taken an eternity.

The elation at having served one year soon turned to despair at the thought of having another four years to go. No matter how I did the calculation, I had still only served twenty per cent of my sentence and I had eighty per cent left to serve. Confronted with a number that was immense, and having endured what I had endured in the first year, I really did wonder whether I would end up making it.

I did not receive education or computer training. I was allowed to go the gym occasionally when we weren't locked down and that was the extent of my lot. I did nuts and bolts in the morning and sometimes in afternoon. Sometimes a group of us would go outside and get away from the mad house that was the unit and do nuts and bolts and have a chat.

For some reason the Bega schoolgirl murderer Leslie Camilleri took an instant dislike to me. I had been at Port Phillip one day when Camilleri tested me and said that I was a cunt and he was going to kill me. I took that threat seriously and thereafter kept my eyes and ears wide open.

I can remember one day sitting in my cell reading with my back to the door. It's funny how, when you are new in jail, you are not a wakeup to all the tricks. I am a bit deaf and another inmate came into my cell, walked up behind me and tapped me on the shoulder. I nearly went through the roof. He said he had heard what Camilleri had said to me and had some advice. Firstly, as I was a bit deaf, it was a good idea not to sit with my back to the door; and secondly I should keep my door snibbed when I was in the cell on my own because most assaults take place in individual cells and I could easily be "got" (jail parlance for being stabbed or beaten) by Camilleri if I left the door unsnibbed. This shook me up a bit and I took his advice on board. Thereafter I didn't sit with my back to the door unless my door was snibbed and I spent more and more time in my cell on my own with the door closed, reading, or watching the television.

Chapter 8

Law and Disorder

Only two things are infinite: the Universe and human stupidity.

ALBERT EINSTEIN

The problem with trying to keep to myself and not attract undue attention was that I "enjoyed" such a high profile among the other prisoners that everyone wanted to unburden themselves to me or to seek legal advice from me. The unit I was placed in was full of psychopaths and sociopaths so you can imagine the quality of the questions that were asked of me.

One thing that has never ceased to amaze me is the extraordinary ignorance among most of the population when it comes to the criminal law. Even those who have had many court room experiences and a lot of contact with the law generally display an almost breathtaking ignorance of the process they are subject to as a lawbreaker. The legal profession generally has an obligation to make sure that those being dealt with under criminal law at least have some rudimentary appreciation of the process that handles them. In reality, most of those convicted walk out of court blissfully ignorant of the details of their penalties. You are given no direction or instruction as to what is required of you in the system; rather, if you make a blue, you are charged – that is how the lesson is learnt.

As for the criminal justice system, lawyers do not take sufficient time to explain, in words of one syllable, the process that dishes out "justice" to a defendant and the means by which the penalty is arrived at. Education is the answer. The number of young men I met in jail who were totally or partially illiterate was astounding. There needs to be real and compulsory education in prison. As a prisoner arrives in the system his educational standard should be assessed and proper, compulsory education provided. As matters stand, there is no real education and nothing is done to educate. If people are ignorant to the degree that they are incapable of reading or comprehending a simple written instruction, they are easier to lie to and mislead, with the result that they are kept in the dark and constantly hoodwinked. Not good enough!

The real problem is that there is not one iota of political will to remedy the situation and society is prepared to let these unfortunates fall through he cracks to a life with no future. Is it any wonder that as soon as these blokes are released they get straight back into drugs and criminal behaviour? There have even been instances where blokes on the train from

Sale to Melbourne have died from an overdose purchased immediately upon their release. Jail sure was a deterrent to them, I don' think!

After a while the assistant gardener at Port Phillip was moved to Ararat Prison to serve the remainder of his sentence and the gardening job came up. I was appointed unit gardener along with Peter Norris Dupas who, as I've already said, is a notorious serial killer. At least I was able to get out into the fresh air a little more now. However, Dupas is one scary customer and I was never comfortable in his company. Dupas is a psychopath in the true sense of the word, in that he is so criminally deranged that he is likely to do anything to anyone at any time without any warning. He has now been convicted of the mutilation murders of three women and is suspected of killing at least that number again, with insufficient evidence to charge him. Dupas is serving life with no minimum, which means he will never be released. He has an extensive criminal history before the murders, all relating to violence against women. Dupas is a glaring example of the total failure of a dysfunctional system that failed to adequately deal with his problems in the beginning or at all. Later he received ridiculously inadequate penalties until he was totally out of control and began his indiscriminate killings.

So the prospect of being in the garden with this monster was a two-edged sword. On the one hand, I was outside in the fresh air; but on the other hand, I was with a psychopath who had gardening tools, including a fork, a pick and a shovel, all of which were potential weapons. I kept my eye very closely on his movements for the entire time we were together.

Amazingly, our relationship managed to be reasonably easy going and we had one thing in common: we were constantly frustrated, in our roles at the gardeners, by the authorities. We wanted to buy some vegetable seeds to sow in our pathetic little vegie garden. This request was refused, even though I was able to pay for the seeds and notwithstanding the fact both Dupas and I were enrolled in the horticulture course at the jail. But our teacher, from Kangan Batman TAFE, was relatively motivated and a good bloke and he insisted that we be allowed to purchase some vegetable seeds through TAFE. The course itself was interesting and helped pass the time, but it was to be of no benefit to me upon my release.

As Dupas and I spent more time together, we even got to the stage of watching gardening shows on TV. Dupas is weird in the true sense of the word, and his antics will be the subject of another book.

Dupas was mates with Ray Edmunds and Paul Gorman the rapist. He was not mates with Camilleri and Chris Hall, another rapist. The friction between the two opposing groups created cliques within the unit. This constant tension occasionally boiled over into violence.

Leslie Camilleri was convicted of a particularly nasty double murder of two schoolgirls in Bega on the Victoria–New South Wales border in 1997. Camilleri and his co-accused, while on an amphetamine-fuelled episode, kidnapped two girls who were hitchhiking. They kept these two girls for days and constantly and sadistically sexually abused them. The whole dreadful incident concluded with the girls' murder – a gutless and callous double slaying. Camilleri is a large man with a brain the size of a pin. His heart is about the same. As they say in jail: Heart as big as a bull-ant's arse!

The problem was that Edmunds, Camilleri and Dupas are all serving life with no minimum and they are going to be in jail with each other for the remainder of their entire lives. The authorities had some difficulty with this and appeared to be constantly hosing down the tension between the two lots of blokes. Edmunds was convicted of a particularly nasty murder of two young lovers by the name of Garry Heywood and Abina Madill at Shepparton in 1966. During his case he had acquired the nickname of "Mr Stinky" and he was and is one of the most notorious prisoners in the Victorian prison system. Edmunds had served twenty years when I first met him. One day I was asking why he had not applied for a minimum of sentence, which he was eligible for after the legislation changed. His reply was that he had done what he had done, he now realised that what he had done was a shocking crime and he was paying the price. Edmunds quite frankly anticipated that he would continue to pay the price until he died. Edmunds was an old man by the time I had met him and I still have trouble rationalising such a penalty.

On any view the crimes of Dupas, Edmunds and Camilleri were about as bad as crimes get. When I look back I still cannot comprehend why I was placed in with criminals such as these.

When considering the particularly vicious crimes these hardened crooks committed, I often wonder whether capital punishment should not be reintroduced. In my view a person who commits offences such as these forfeits their right to life. They have most certainly forfeited the right to remain in our society. One therefore wonders why society should throw good money after bad at what is essentially a futile exercise – namely, keeping somebody alive who will not be of any benefit to society and will never be a part of society again. Capital punishment is an option that all governments will refuse to canvass because, I believe, if it were put to a referendum, it would be endorsed. My views on this will no doubt create a furore. But remember, I have lived with this human refuse and have been given the opportunity to reach my point of view from first-hand experience.

I should be very clear that when I talk of capital punishment I differentiate between the Dupases or Camilleris of this world and other "ordinary" murderers. Remember, most murders are domestic in nature or the killer is known to the deceased. Other so-called "underworld" murders do not fit into the same category either. If you are a career criminal and you end up on the wrong end of a "knock", bad luck. After all, it is an occupational hazard. These two categories of murders do not come close to the callous, brutal killing of defenceless women and children and it is my view, after living with these low-lifes, that no good is served in keeping them on this planet. Capital punishment is justified in these cases.

The other question on which society must make some hard decisions is the thorny one of drugs. Drugs in jail are rampant. Anything you want, you can have – provided you can pay for it. Officers bring drugs into jail – end of story. We will have all of the authorities duck and weave as much as they like but numerous officers have been convicted of introducing contraband – whether it be drugs or alcohol or other items such as pornography – into jail and the proportion of officers committing those offences is extremely high.

If drug use is a health issue then the law must be changed to remove the sanctions that now apply. If not, then all persons must be dealt with equally, and that includes sporting officials who cover up a drug scandal. If legislation regards the use of drugs, or anything to do with drugs, as a criminal offence then there must be zero tolerance. At the moment no one seems to be able to reconcile the two opposing camps. One way or the other, the present system cannot prevail because the two positions are contradictory. If drugs are a criminal offence then everybody should be dealt with equally under the law. After all, the basic tenet of the law is that everybody must be dealt with equally. The only problem is that some are dealt with more equally than others!

I call on the responsible politicians to extract their digits and do something about this; otherwise we will continue to have this ridiculous situation where somebody with no dough and no education is charged with drugs and ends up in jail while league footballers are admitting to drug use and not being sanctioned in any way – including by a clearly compliant police force. The two cannot run together.

As I finish writing this book a report has just been released by the Australian National Council on Drugs that says more money should be spent on drug treatment programs aimed at keeping people out of jail There's nothing cheap about sending someone to jail. It costs the taxpayer between $50,000 and $75,000 a year, according to the council. They say that more than 25,000 people are doing time around Australia and 60 per cent of offenders report some level of drug use during their sentence. This report is a step in the right direction, but it remains to be seen whether anything will change as a result.

Life at Port Phillip droned on. The boredom was stifling. The futility was stifling. The absurdity of the whole system was stifling. I constantly felt overwhelmed by my situation and I started to suffer panic attacks again. There was no logical reason for me to suffer these panic attacks but I did. There was no logical reason for me to suffer depression but I did. I spoke to the doctor about both, and the doctor's panacea was to prescribe antidepressants but I refused. I treated myself by increasing my running and by involving myself in as much physical exercise as I possibly could and this overcame the panic attacks and depression to some degree. Winston

Churchill described depression as "the black dog" … how true that is.

I remained in maximum security in protection from protection for over two years until somebody finally asked me why I had signed myself into protection. I had arranged with the screws who ran the gym, against all the rules, to allow some former clients of mine to be in the gym at the same time as I was. At least now I was able to talk to some people I knew and it was during one of these chats that I was advised that I was supposed to have signed a written form seeking protection and if I hadn't, all I had to do was ask for a form to sign myself out of protection into mainstream. I was further told by these experienced prisoners that I would have no problems in mainstream, and never did have. And it was their view that the only reason I had been placed in protection was to have it effectively stuck up me by the authorities and by the coppers as a payback. I immediately went to see Sentence Management.

As an aside, the screws who allowed these rule breaches to occur were later charged with drug trafficking and other corrupt activities. Do you ever see these cases reported in the media? No!

This time I was seen not by Mr Orr but by a bloke named Dennis Barnes. Mr Barnes is an ex-screw who sits on Sentence Management. I pointed out to him that I now knew that I had been placed in protection against my will and that I wanted to sign myself out. Barnes said to me that I could not do that. I said that they had "got" me once but now I knew my rights and, if not moved immediately, I would issue habeas corpus. "What is that?" was his reply. I advised that it was an ancient writ available to anybody wrongly imprisoned (its literal meaning being "thou shalt have the body"). Sentence Management had twenty-four hours to move me or I would take out such a writ. Barnes left the room, came back and said I would be moved to mainstream but not until the next afternoon because I was being moved to Borrowdale, a brand-new unit where I would have a single cell on my own from the time I was moved there. I was prepared to wait.

While in Sirius East for the first few months I was subjected to maximum security within a maximum security unit. That is, I was ordered to move cells every two weeks. Why? you may ask. Quite simply, I don't know. I kept asking why I was being moved all the time and was met with the reply "You are being moved for security reasons." It made no sense to me. It was a small unit – the smallest unit in the jail – and each inmate knew where everybody lived. Each time I was moved, I was put in a cell that was putrid. I would then have to empty the cell and repeat the cleaning ritual that I had perfected at MAP.

I was lucky enough not to get sick in jail, probably because of my strict hygiene regime. The jails are rife with hepatitis, AIDS and plenty of other diseases. Of course, hepatitis is many times over the national average in jail due to drug use and the sharing of infected needles. Because the authorities simply deny the widespread use of drugs in jail, they don't allow the provision of clean needles. So if you are a junkie who is sentenced to a term of imprisonment, you are being sentenced to a term of imprisonment together with a dose of hepatitis if you don't already have it. That is a given – there is no ifs, buts or maybes about it.

There is also the issue of homosexuality and rape, which are also rife and again are denied or knowingly ignored. The Commissioner's refusal to allow condoms in jail is further evidence of a system in denial. By way of example there was a young bloke in Sirius East giving head jobs in return for other prisoners' medication. These acts were performed in full view of the officers' station. Another young bloke was being forced, by another, older prisoner who was serving a lengthy sentence for rapes, to partake in anal sex. This same older prisoner repeatedly asked to be moved into a two man cell whenever a young prisoner came to the unit. The pretext given was that he was helping the young bloke through a difficult time. The inevitable complaint of rape would always come from every young prisoner a few days later, resulting in the young prisoner being moved. What sanction did the rapist suffer? Nothing.

There were certain officers who asked me if there was "anything" I wanted (meaning drugs). No, there wasn't. It was made clear to me that drugs may be purchased from these officers. I did not take them up on their offer as I was drug free and had been since my arrest. It is now eight years since

I was arrested and I have not returned one "dirty" (positive) urine sample in that time.

On another occasion one of the prisoners in the maintenance gang came to the unit to have a look at the exercise bike and I got talking to him. He asked me if I wanted any cocaine. I asked, "As a matter of interest, how much do you have?" He said, "A half." I said, "What, a half a gram?" He said, "No, a half ounce." I couldn't believe it. He wrote down some banking particulars for me and said that once the requisite amount – $4000 for half an ounce – had been deposited the drugs would be delivered to me. I immediately gave those particulars to Detective Inspector Di Santo of the Ethical Standards Department of Victoria Police, together with the paper with the prisoner's handwriting on it – and guess what? Nothing was ever done about it. Needless to say, I did not take the bloke up on his offer but I was surprised at the quantity of drugs he had available. Half an ounce is a lot of drugs to have – especially for a prisoner. By the way, the price was double the going rate on the outside.

As promised I was moved to Borrowdale and, boy, was I glad to get out of Sirius East. In fact, there were even a couple of friendly faces in Borrowdale. One was JR ("Not guilty") Ridgeway – an old, old client of mine and not a bad bloke. He introduced me to all the other shakers and movers in the unit and my life suddenly became one hell of a lot better.

The big difference between protection and mainstream was that there were not so many cliques in the unit but there was a lot more violence. Punch-ons were a regular occurrence. On one occasion, there had been a punch-on between a couple of prisoners and we were being locked down. A bloke called Nathan Berry was standing by his cell door when the officers came along to lock us down. Nathan said, "Why are we being locked down? It's all over." The screw told him to get fucked and get into the cell. Nathan lost it, jumped at the screw and grabbed him around the neck then started wrestling with him and trying to choke him. Needless to say, he got the kicking of all time and was taken off to the slot.

On another occasion a young Aboriginal prisoner came into the unit and he was clearly not well mentally. He was screaming and shouting and carrying on from the minute he walked into the unit until he left, which was not long afterwards. I was mopping the top tier as he was being directed to a cell. One minute I was bending over minding my own business and the next, as he walked past, he delivered a flying kick at me. Luckily I saw it out of the corner of my eye and jumped away, at the same time fending him off with the mop. He went into his cell yelling and screaming all the while. The next minute the television came flying out the door and over the edge of the tier down onto the ground floor where it shattered. You could hear everything in his cell smashing.

One of the screws raced up and slammed the door into his cell and locked the unit down. Why the unit needed to be locked down I do not know. Borrowdale, being a new unit, had different ventilation gaps at the bottom of each cell door.

You could lie on your stomach and see the rest of the unit, and I could see this prisoner's cell from mine. Then the riot squad appeared – yes, just like you see on the TV: helmets with visors, clear riot shields and a long baton – and I soon knew why we had been locked down. There were about six of them and they came into the unit and stood by the offender's cell door. One of the other screws came up and unsnibbed the door for them.

The riot squad started banging their shields with their batons like they do on TV and raced into this small cell. The screaming that followed was blood curdling. I was lying on my stomach watching all of this and then I saw the young Aborigine dragged out by the riot blokes, covered in blood, barely conscious. He had copped a severe beating. He was then thrown head first down the steel steps to the ground floor. He was removed and not seen again.

We remained locked down for some considerable period as there was a blood spill in the unit. We were not allowed out until a specialised group had come in and cleaned up the blood. This is what happens to you in jail if you step out of line.

The incident I've just recounted raises yet another question. The mental health system in Victoria has been gutted to such an extent that there are no facilities available for troubled souls like this young bloke. They are now placed in jail, and a more inappropriate placing I cannot imagine. Mr Kennett is now head of Beyond Blue, a body that deals with mental illness, particularly depression. I bet Mr Kennett has never seen the result of his government's actions, filling jails with the mentally ill. I wonder when it was that Mr Kennett had his "road to Damascus" moment and saw the error of his previous ways. Too late for many, now inappropriately banged up in the prison system. Well done Jeff!

The other thing that amazed me about being in mainstream was the drug culture. The big ticket item was Immovane, which is a very strong sleeping tablet. There were a number crooks in this unit serving over twenty years for murder (including Matthew Wales, the so-called society murderer, who used to cut my hair). These blokes would go into a cell of a new inmate who had never been in custody before and the deal went something like this.

The new chum would be told, not asked, that he could be prescribed Immovane for three nights because he was a first timer and would probably have difficulty sleeping. That new prisoner would then be told to present to the doctor that day. He would be prescribed the sleepers, which would be dispensed on pill parade that night. The prisoner would secrete the tablets under his tongue and later give them to the other prisoner. For each night of the prescription he would give his pills to an inmate with a promise that they would square up by buying him canteen on canteen day.

Well, of course, the inevitable would then happen. The newcomer would be lashed (not paid) on canteen day. He would then arc up about not being paid and would blame these crooks, complaining that he had given them the tablets and they had given him nothing – whereupon he would get a belting from the blokes who had received his medication and had then refused to pay. The new bloke would appear on muster with a black eye, a bruised face and possibly a split lip. The prisoner would be asked by the screws what happened, and he would say he walked into the door. The crooks serving the long sentences had their "lollies" and the new bloke would have nothing for his troubles except for a smack in the mouth.

On one particular night, one long-serving crook was so off his face on Immovane that, as he was going up the stairs to his cell for muster, he fell face forward onto the steel stairs, smashed his head, lay there for a minute or so until he could regain his senses, staggered upstairs and walked along the top holding onto the rails until he got to his cell, then muster was conducted as if nothing had happened.

This went on and on and on, to the point where I got so sick of it. One night, the same crook was walking around with about eight to ten Immovane on him. I said to one of the screws, "Aren't you ever going to do anything about this?" I indicated the particular prisoner as he walked in and out of each new inmate's cell collecting. The screw just looked at me and said, "Piss off." That's the attitude you get in jail. This particular inmate was collecting six to eight Immovane a day. He was a big man and had developed a big tolerance to Immovane but he was still effectively sleeping away his sentence. I suppose, on reflection, it's not a bad way to go:

you don't have to confront your demons. Talk about "Life...
Be out of it!"

One wonders what the hell is going on here. Why aren't
more positive urine samples returned if this behaviour is going
on like I say it is? The answer to that is very clear: there are
few truly random drug tests taken in jail. Each jail is required
to take a certain number of urine samples, and a certain percentage of those samples must be clean. If there are too many
positive samples the private jails suffer a financial penalty. To
get around this, the powers that be at Port Phillip target those
they know are not using drugs. On your drug sheet it states
whether your sample is "random" or "targeted". My tests were
always "targeted". I was constantly tested and when I walked
into the medical centre to be tested there would be all the
same blokes – namely, all those the jail knew were not using.
Only the clean prisoners would be tested. This process provides a nice bunch of clean samples and the threshold is not
breached. Group 4, who were then running the jail, would
not be financially penalised. In addition, it would make good
reading for the politicians that dirty drugs tests were down in
the jail system. The whole deal is a total joke.

At least now that I was in mainstream, life was a little easier.
But the greatest bone of contention for all prisoners was the
question of lockdowns. The Corrections Act states that if a
prisoner is locked down for a day or any part thereof for an
emergency or a security reason, then the prisoner receives a

credit of four days for every day locked down – that is, four days off his sentence.

The company that runs Port Phillip could not run a pie cart! The joint is a complete and utter shambles and lock-downs are constant. During the period I was at Port Phillip which was three years approximately, I endured lockdowns of varying lengths on 132 of those days. You may ask: How much time did I receive off my sentence as a credit for these lockdowns? Not one minute!

The lockdown issue became so contentious that a bloke by the name of Andy Bogle from the Commissioner's office at Corrections Victoria came and visited me with a view to trying to sort out the mess. I said to him that we were constantly locked down and he replied that Mr Anderson was reviewing the situation and I ought put in writing to him all about the lockdowns. As a lawyer one is taught to pay attention to detail. I was aware of the legislation relating to lockdowns and I had also read the Hansard (transcript of parliamentary debates) relating to the credits to be given. The parliamentary theory was that if you suffered harsh or unusual punishment then you received a discount off your sentence as a result of that. The overwhelming theory is supposedly that you go to jail as punishment, not for punishment, and unforeseen lockdowns are additional punishment.

I kept a contemporaneous note of each lockdown as it took place and my notes on the lockdowns were meticulous. I wrote to Mr Anderson detailing each and every lockdown and its duration. Anderson wrote back denying that some of the lockdowns had taken place as they were not on the prison records. Just imagine not keeping a record of seven hundred blokes being locked down all at one time. It beggars belief. I wrote back to Mr Anderson pointing out that I had made a note of these lockdowns as they took place and, frankly, I didn't care what his records said; mine were correct and his were wrong. This was symptomatic of the way the jail was run. Matters of such import as lockdowns were not recorded.

You were never told when a lockdown is going to occur. And you were never told how long each lockdown was likely to be, so you sat there at 8.30 each morning of the lockdown, wondering, wondering, wondering when you'll be let out, and the door may or may not open.

A lot of this may sound disjointed, but that was precisely what life in jail is like. The prison guards try to keep you as wrong-footed as possible. The idea is not to let you get yourself into any routine where you know exactly what is going to happen and begin to feel comfortable – heaven forbid!

In mainstream the time allocated for me to go for a run was from 10 till 11 each morning and it took me nine months to get permission to go to another unit, where there was a 300 metre track, for that particular hour. So many times I would be sitting in my cell in my running gear at 9.45, doing my stretching in preparation for the run, the cell door not having been opened at 8.30, 9 o'clock, 9.30… Then, of course, 10 o'clock comes and goes – no gym, no run, nothing. And you are not told a thing. Running each day was the most important thing to me: that was what I looked forward to, that was what I lived for. When the door wasn't opened at 10 o'clock, my day was effectively over. What else to do for the rest of the day? The best you could do was walk backwards and forwards in a very small garden. Maybe you could do a little bit of weight work on the one gym station in the unit, which was monopolised by the long-term prisoners. It was very difficult to get a go on that machine.

All in all, the frustration that arose from these lockdowns was immense. Finally a bloke called Steve Pavic took the Corrections Commissioner to court over the lockdowns and lost. The Court of Criminal Appeal in the Supreme Court of Victoria effectively said that they were not prepared to interfere in the administration of the prison system. What a pathetic, gutless copout that is. If prisoners cannot seek redress from the Supreme Court for wrongs done to them by the administration of the prison system, then what hope is there? The answer is that there is no hope whatsoever for prisoners and this is yet another example of the complete failure of the system to rehabilitate anybody.

It is often said that a healthy body equals a healthy mind. In jail I did everything possible to keep my body healthy and at every turn the authorities endeavoured to stymie my attempts. Often, when going to the other unit for my run, upon presenting my movement slip, I would have some smart-arse screw say to me, "Well, if it was up to me I wouldn't let you go in here to run." My answer to that was, "I have a movement slip. Please open the gate." It was most certainly not what I felt like saying but it was what I did say because if I'd arced up then I would have been barred entry.

I became fitter and fitter and my reading proceeded. I was lucky in that my wife made sure that I had a full list of visitors to see me each week. I was also lucky in that a number of my lawyer mates stuck by me and occasionally, when they were visiting jail, they would call me out for a professional visit as well. That meant that I had my full quota of three visits per week plus the odd professional visit. This made life at least bearable as surprisingly some prisoners get no visits at all and others have only one or two visits a year. Additionally, I was very lucky in that my sister paid for my phone, my canteen spend and my newspapers everyday for the entirety of sentence. I read each and every newspaper from cover to cover, even the obituaries. I read every book I could get my hands on. I had a constant stream of books posted to me by friends and well wishers, some just appearing out of the blue. Occasionally I would receive a letter from somebody I hadn't heard from for years. You cannot begin to believe how good you feel when something like that happens. It was fantastic and made me feel that maybe I'm not the worst person in the world.

My family visited me every Tuesday and my mum and dad and sister visited me every Thursday. I lived to see my kids and it tore my heart out every Tuesday night when they left. There were friends I rang on a daily basis and with whom I chatted for the permissible time, which was twenty minutes, after which the phone would automatically cut out. It made my day to be able to ring normal people from the outside world and have sensible discussions with them. I thank those people from the bottom of my heart for all their support. They know who they are and they don't need to be named.

I started seeing Sentence Management on a more regular basis. Each time, I asked to be moved from maximum security to a country jail. Each time I asked for a reason as to why I was still in maximum security and not in some country jail. There are other lawyers in jail, and they were sent to country jails almost immediately. I was left in maximum security from November 2001 until February 2005. Why?

I finally saw Sentence Management in December 2004 and really laid it on the line. I had had a gutful of Port Phillip and I wanted written reasons from them as to why they continually refused to move me to even a medium-security jail. I asked for reasons in writing because once I had them in writing, I would be able to review Sentence Management's decision in the Supreme Court and they knew that. On reflection I should have made this request earlier because it had the desired effect. I was immediately given a B rating, which meant I could go to a country jail.

I was moved in early January 2005 to Fulham Correctional Centre near West Sale in eastern Victoria. Fulham is a medium and minimum security jail – and if I thought Port Phillip was a bun fight, it wasn't even in the game compared with the disorganised shit fight that passes as Fulham Correctional Centre. Fulham had the reputation of being a jail awash with drugs. That was an understatement. I have never seen so many drugs – on the outside or on the inside – as there are at Fulham. Once again that will be denied vigorously by everybody to do with the prison system but it is the case, whether or not they like it to be known.

Even the trip to Fulham was an interesting experience, to say the least. There is supposedly no smoking on any of the vans when you are being moved. What a lot of crap that is. The first thing that happens is that before blokes leave, a lot of them carry contraband by "booting" it. That means they wrap whatever they want to take with them in cling wrap and stick it up their rectum so it won't be discovered. Yes, they stick it up their bum! We got on the bus after being strip-searched and having all our property searched. The first thing the blokes do is drop their strides and start fishing around in their arse for their tobacco and other items – matches, bits of matchbox to strike the matches on, papers, the works. On one occasion I even saw a bloke remove a teaspoon from his arse to mix up some heroin!

After a smoke-fuelled trip the bus finally arrived at Fulham. I was called out first and was marched into a room where the operations manager and the officer who was in charge of security for the jail gave me a dressing down. I was not to give any legal advice. I was not to read any legal papers for inmates. I was not to discuss any legal matters with anybody.

Did I understand that? Yes, but the chances of that happening were a million to one. From the very minute I arrived at Port Phillip I had been asked to read blokes court papers. People would come up and ask me questions about their case or the law generally. Peter Dupas had me give detailed advice in relation to his murder cases, and that continued at Fulham – but more so.

Fulham is an open jail. There are no walls between units and it is very easy for people to walk in and out of the units. They did this with monotonous regularity. So much for keeping to myself! I was first placed in the induction unit, where we again had to go through all the introductory nonsense about jails.

At Port Phillip I had been what is known as a "prison listener". You became a prison listener by doing a course that effectively taught you how to be a counsellor for other prisoners. I thoroughly enjoyed this aspect of jail life as it gave me a lot more freedom. I was paid in kind on a fortnightly basis: I received two pouches of White Ox tobacco, two packets of papers, two jars of Nescafe coffee and a packet of biscuits. Not being a smoker, the tobacco was as good as currency and each week I was able to swap my tobacco for canteen items, thereby making my life a little bit easier and more pleasant. The idea of prison listeners is that there are often matters that prisoners want to discuss but will not discuss either with other officers or prison medical staff. Often I would be asked to go and talk to prisoners about how they were feeling, about their families, trepidation about their court cases, fear of the unknown after they had received a sentence. These sort of requests invariably happened on a Friday night when blokes came back from court to jail and had had a bad result.

One poor old bloke I remember in particular was Old Rick. Old Rick was a drunk from St Kilda and had got into a blue with his drinking mate and had killed him. It was a manslaughter if I had ever seen one. Rick was seventy-two and he could not get it into his mind that he was not going to be convicted of murder. I kept talking and talking to him. The night before he was due to go to court only for a mention, not even for his committal, he was in a real state. I was taken in to see him by the screws after lockdown. I sat for about an hour with him in his cell, and he told me he could see no end to his problems. He was an old man with no future and was terrified of spending the rest of his life in jail. After about an hour, I thought I had hosed him down to the point where he understood what was going to happen the next day and that in the long run he would be OK.

The next morning I heard muster being conducted. The morning muster is what's called a hands-on-trap muster – that is, you stand behind the trap door on your cell and identify yourself when it is opened. Rick's cell was a few cells down from mine. I heard the trap open and the screws scream out "code black". A code black is a deceased person. Old Rick had seen no end to his plight. After I left, he had packed up his cell, folded everything neatly on his bed, then brought the plastic waste bin over, slashed his wrists, bled himself out into the waste bin then fallen onto the floor and died. I was very sad at this unnecessary death. However, that is jail: you see lots of things you don't want to see in jail. Why he was there for what was essentially a drunken brawl by a couple old winos, I don't know.

At Fulham, though, the prison listeners were a different kettle of fish. Because of the drug situation there, they had to be completely upfront about the state of play. They made no bones about it, no covering up there. They said, "We will help you with any problems except drug debts. And be told: at Fulham if you don't pay for your drugs, you will be hurt and hurt badly." Those comments were prescient, as I saw more violence over drugs at Fulham than I had seen in the whole of my sentence at a maximum-security facility.

Once in the induction unit at Fulham I had to undergo occupation health and safety training and basic first aid training, all of which I had undertaken at Port Phillip – but that didn't matter, it had to be done again. I applied to become a prison listener and, notwithstanding that I was the busiest and the most requested listener at Port Phillip, I was told that I was not suitable to be a prison listener at Fulham. To this day I don't know why I was inappropriate, but so be it. I decided to get on with my time at Fulham. At least down there, there was a big gymnasium and there was a running track of nearly a kilometre, where I could go for virtually the entire time we were out of our cells. This was as good as it could get in prison and I was starting to feel more relaxed immediately.

People said to me that my co-accused, Carl Urbanec, was also at Fulham and that there may be trouble. On my first afternoon off the bus I bumped into Urbanec. His reaction was one of friendship and sympathy. He kept saying to me, "Why are you in jail for this? You had nothing to do with this. It was our gig." In his view, I had not been a player in the importation. That was a relief as that was the only piece of aggravation that could potentially have caused me problems at Fulham, as far as I was aware.

What I was not aware of was that another prisoner, whom I didn't know from a bar of soap, was making allegations about my behaviour with an alleged friend of his who was a former client of mine. He was running around saying that I owed this client $40,000 and that I had stolen it from him and he had my trust account receipts to prove it. The only problem with that piece of nonsense is that if I had a trust account receipt for it then his "mate" would not have lost the money.

Chapter 9
Day Out

If you can fill the unforgiving minute
With sixty seconds worth of distance run,
Yours is the Earth and everything that's in it,
And – what is more – you'll be a man my son!

IF, RUDYARD KIPLING

On my second day at Fulham I was summoned to see a bloke by the name of Big George Da Costa, who was in for a murder. The authorities think they run Fulham. That is a wrong. Big George runs Fulham. And when I was called to see him, everybody was most apprehensive about me going. I went, however, and George indicated to me that some good people in Griffith and Mildura who respected me for the work I had carried out for them over the years had asked him to look after me and make sure I was OK. Over the years I had done a stack of work for the Italians from Griffith and Mildura and I was relieved indeed at this comment. Big George went on to say that, if I had a problem, I should come and see him – but as far as he was concerned and from the enquiries he had made, I had no problems and that would remain the situation.

Fulham is a complete mad house. It is run by people who are former farmers from the area and who have not been able to make a go of farming, so the next step down from milking cows at 4 in the morning is to mustering crooks at 6.30. I could go on and on about the idiocy that pervades Fulham but a few examples will suffice.

The first is a young bloke by the name of Matt (not his real name). Matt was a local who had been convicted of culpable driving. The evidence given on his plea was that he was socially inept and was easily influenced by other people. The learned trial judge in the County Court who sentenced Matt, firstly wrongly directed herself as to the law by stating that drinking and speeding in a motor vehicle were aggravating circumstances of the offence of culpable driving. Anybody who has bothered to read the Crimes Act as far as it relates to culpable driving will see that that is incorrect. Speeding and alcohol are elements of culpable driving, not aggravating circumstances. Notwithstanding Her Honour's incorrect self-direction, she sentenced Matt to a substantial sentence for culpable driving and ordered that, due to his social pliability, he serve his sentence at the youth section at Fulham, which is known as "Nalu".

Herein lies a fundamental problem with the system: If Her Honour had bothered to ask anybody or if any evidence regarding rating of prisoners and their placement had been available, she would have been told that before one can be considered for Nalu Unit, you must have one year left of your sentence, not six or seven as Matt was staring at. Such evidence was not available to Her Honour, with the result that she was shooting in the dark about what would happen to Matt once he was imprisoned. Matt was placed in mainstream at Fulham. Being young and socially inept, it wasn't long before Matt was moved out of the units into a lodge with older, more experienced and more hardened criminals than he would ever be.

The lodges at Fulham are the next step down the scale. The accommodation is for eight blokes, each with their own bedrooms, and the prison supplies the food which you then cook. Many long-termers live in the lodges. Matt was employed in the gardening unit, driving the ride-on mower around Fulham. He was immediately recruited as a drug courier around the jail and there he is to this day, merrily driving the mower and doing his deliveries.

An additional annoying factor for Matt was that he was represented by Legal Aid on his plea. He naturally requested that Legal Aid fund his appeal to the Court of Criminal Appeal against the severity of his sentence. He was refused legal aid for an appeal. This beggars belief because, as I said, the learned sentencing judge had fundamentally misdirected herself as to the law. If anybody at Legal Aid had even bothered to turn their mind to it, it would have been patently obvious that Matt had gold-plated grounds for appeal. Unfortunately legal aid was refused. Matt had nowhere to go and there he is now, a million miles away from the Nalu Unit for youth and serving a sentence with hardened criminals who can only influence him to his, and in the long run the community's, detriment.

Why the judge did not call evidence about placement, I do not know. Over the years it has occurred to me that this is a glaring fault in the system. Why don't people from Corrections commissions give evidence to courts about offenders' placement, what rating (risk) will be applied to any given prisoner, where they should be placed, what rehabilitation (theoretically) is available and what would be happening to these people for the remainder of their sentence? Surely a sentencing judge, who is the only person in possession of all the facts, should be the one who sets out a sentencing plan for offenders, not somebody down the track from Sentence Management or Corrections, who has merely read a half baked précis of what has happened and what the judge said.

After I had been at Fulham for a while I was finally moved to the minimum-security section known as "The Cottages". The Cottages are four-man huts where you each have your own bedroom. The big change for me was that the furniture was not bolted to the floor and I was able, at long last, to move the furniture around to suit myself. I know this sounds a small thing but after four years of living with everything bolted to the floor it was a welcome relief! There was a shared bathroom and small laundry.

My favourite thing was that there was a kitchen with the necessary equipment for cooking – knives, forks, saucepans, etc. After three years at Port Phillip, this was luxury indeed and I immediately took to cooking as much as I could with the limited resources available. We were given a budget of $37.50 per week for each prisoner or $150 per cottage to plan your menu for the week and order accordingly. When you are being ripped off to the extent of nearly $19 per kilo for lamb chops, $37.50 does not go far! I became rather expert at cooking with pulses and other cheap ingredients. I had never made many cakes but by the time I left Fulham I was a dab hand at fruit cakes, chocolate éclairs and even pavlovas. My kids still enjoy chocolate muffins in their lunches.

That was the good part of being in the cottages. The bad part was that you didn't get to choose who you lived with and once again the screws made life very difficult by virtue of the people they put in with me. I got on well with one bloke, Cam ("the Captain") Strachan. But we also lived with at psychopath, Bobby ("the Batsman") Pickford. Bob was in for a double thrill kill and had served a quick twenty-two years. He just did not get with the program at all, he was a serial masturbator and would sell his soul for a girlie magazine (which of course was strictly forbidden). Poor Bob has no idea, and I hate to think what's going to happen when he is ultimately released on parole. As Bob could not remotely cope with living in a cottage, I hate to think how he will go on parole. Bob was not on a leave programme, did not work outside the jail or have any interaction with anyone outside our cottage. Bob's one task was to empty the cottage's rubbish bins daily. What terrific rehabilitation for a killer!

While on the topic of parole, when people muck up on parole, as they invariably do, why is the Parole Board never taken to task about their poor choices and the poor directions given to crooks who are released on parole? The Parole Board is virtually untouchable – you are not allowed representation before the Parole Board and decisions cannot be challenged. And the Court of Appeal backs the philosophy that you cannot challenge the Parole Board, its decisions or its findings. This major fault in the system needs to be addressed as a matter of urgency because many, many relevant matters are not put before the Parole Board. Such as the example of young Trent.

Trent was working with me in the property store at Fulham. The property store is supposed to be a position of trust where you work away from the main body of the jail and you are left virtually alone to do your job, with one screw and one administrative officer running the place. It is a busy job, particularly on escort days when there is an influx of new prisoners. You can work until seven or eight o'clock at night, which suited me down to the ground because the days went very quickly. I must give credit where it's due: the officer who was running the property store at the time was more than happy to let me have my run every morning at ten thirty so that I could keep up my physical fitness regime.

When I started in the property store, I noticed young Trent sticking his head into various prisoners' property boxes and he told me he was merely taking stuff out for the prisoner whose box it was and would deliver the items to them. These items were refused items, such as new runners, CDs and other odds and ends. It transpired that this was not the case at all and that young Trent was stealing from those boxes and selling the product of his theft for cigarettes. I told him that I did not want anything to do with this and whenever I saw him sniffing around a property box I headed in the other direction. The inevitable happened: Trent was caught and marched off to the slot for the remainder of his sentence. The interesting aspect of this episode was that Trent had appeared before the Parole Board about a month before he was caught for theft. He had been granted parole and was due for release a couple weeks after his apprehension for these numerous thefts.

One would have thought logically that, if a prisoner who had been granted parole in relation to an armed robbery had been caught for theft, it would be a relevant matter to put before the Parole Board. But no, the opposite happened. Trent was taken to the slot (solitary) where he remained for the last two weeks of his sentence, and he was then released on parole with nobody being any the wiser.

When word of Trent's behaviour leaked out, many prisoners asked to check their property boxes – and guess what?

A heap of property was missing. Once again there was an attempted cover-up of the true position.

The Operations Manager, Mr Walker, had previously been the Operations Manager at Barwon Prison, which is the State's 'Super Max' jail and he brought a Super Max philosophy with him to Fulham, which is a medium and minimum security jail. From the time he arrived at Fulham he singled me out as a person who needed to be given a particularly hard time. Up until Walker's arrival I had had an uneventful period at Fulham and time was starting to move a little quicker. I had my own room, which I had set up as best I could with my books, my TV, a computer (which I had finally been allowed after three years) and my music. I was working as hard as I could at studying British and Australian History and English Literature. Needless to say, I had a lot of books in my room and while, strictly speaking, because of my studies and the amount of time I spent reading I was exceeding the number of books allowed, everybody was happy to let me have those books.

As soon as Mr Walker arrived however, two things happened. First of all, he came into my room and said "All them books is going." The minute he uttered those words I knew I had a problem. I asked on what basis were they going. He said, "You've got too many." I explained why I needed all the books. I explained that some were poetry, some were literature, I had a few dictionaries and a thesaurus, and I had history textbooks. He said I didn't need all of those books. I said that I would do a deal and that if he could tell me the date of the second Sikh war and the dates of the Wars of the Roses (not the movie) then I would put all the books in my property. Walker stopped and looked at me, eyeballing me face to face, as I stood my ground. In the end he said, "Just stick your books out of sight."

That was a small win but that small win was soon to backfire on me. The question of leaves prior to your release loom large in a prisoner's life. In the State of Victoria, if you have been sentenced to a term of imprisonment of three years or more to serve, then for the last year of your sentence, you are entitled to leaves. The first three leaves are to be escorted in the presence of an officer to the local area. If you conclude these leaves without incident you are entitled to unescorted leaves for the purposes of working, up to a maximum of seventy-two hours in the month before your release. The whole idea of leaves is obvious: after a long sentence you need all the help you can to re-integrate into society.

The Corrections Act provides for two, and two only, preconditions for you to be granted leaves. One, that you have been of good behaviour; and two, that you are in the last year of your sentence. There are no conditions subject to the legislation at all. This does not, however, stop the Corrections Commissioner, Mr Anderson, imposing his own additional conditions and further it does not stop Mr Walker habitually making a decision that he is not going to give leaves. And guess what, as per usual in jail, "Get fucked. You are just not getting them" was his response to me.

I now call on Mr Anderson, Mr John Myer (the Governor at Fulham) and Mr Walker to furnish me with their reasons as to why I was only ever granted one-day unescorted leaves to Melbourne and why I was refused any overnight leaves before my release.

Every reason that Mr Walker put forward as to why I was refused overnight leaves was false. Firstly, that I did not need to seek work: Wrong, I had been struck off as a solicitor and had no work to come home to. I needed to track down some form of employment and that opportunity was denied me. Secondly, that I was married and had a family to go home to: Wrong, by that stage my marriage had failed and I did not even have anywhere to stay. Furthermore, unsurprisingly my first three escorted leaves took place without incident. My fourth leave, my first unescorted leave to Melbourne, was approved by Fulham and for reasons that still have not been explained to me, Miss Vicky Ryan at Sentence Management refused it. I hit the roof as the leave was cancelled only two days before it was to take place. To this day I have not been given an adequate reason for my leaves being cancelled. The public again must ask whether it wants the prisoners who are released into society to be properly reintegrated or not. Not only were the leaves not allowed, I was then refused any leaves at all for the next three months. Despite constant requests I have never been provided with any explanation for such actions.

I had been an exemplary prisoner, there were no incidents on my records, there was no drug use, no violence, no back-chat, there was nothing. In other words, if ever there was a prisoner who ought to have been given his leaves, it was me. The only reason I didn't get leaves was because Mr Walker didn't like me and Mr Myers refused to discuss the matter with me.

I give this example because once again the community has got to decide whether the parliaments who make the laws are the ones to be listened to or some bureaucrat who is flat out spelling his own name is allowed to have this sort of power over somebody's life. In my view it is an outrage that, after four years, your emotions are still being played with to this degree by the powers that be. All of the people mentioned above – namely Messrs Anderson, Myers and Walker and Ms Ryan – can say what they like but the reality is that my leaves were refused for no reason.

Mr Walker arrived at Fulham with a fearsome reputation. "The Barrel" was a man to be reckoned with and the first thing he did when he arrived was order a complete search of the whole jail. We were locked down for days while this took place. The only catch was that I was working in the laundry when these searches took place and I could see all the comings and goings at my cottage from the laundry. Rather than find any contraband there, a prison officer who still remains unknown stole a CD-ROM from me during this search. I was not happy about this and had a lot to say about it. Nobody denied that the theft had taken place, but it took some months for the prison to finally pay me compensation for the theft.

The basis on which Fulham operates is that if the authorities muck you around for long enough, you will get sick of whatever it is you are pursuing and give it away. Not in my case: I was furious that a prison officer had stolen from me and there was no way I was letting this go.

These particular incidents should give you some idea of what sort of a prison Fulham was and while, yes, I was able to go for a run each day and, yes, I was allowed to have visitors on the weekend, it was in a lot of ways more frustrating than being in Port Phillip because everything was so slapdash that the anxiety of never knowing what was going to happen next was upon us nearly every day.

One Saturday evening, we were locked down an hour early. Why? Because there was a farewell for one of the officers! How good is that? I bet Corrections Victoria didn't know that the entire jail of over 700 blokes was locked down early so all the screws could get on the piss in Sale to say farewell to one of their own. What a joke.

I cannot finish this book without a general observation about jail rehabilitation and the lies that are constantly fed to the general public as to how successful rehabilitation in jail is.

In a court, before a crook is sentenced, his defence counsel stands up and quacks on about "rehabilitation", his client's prospects for same and usually, that a long sentence will be crushing, thereby diluting chances of rehabilitation. Sentencing judges make all the suitably po-faced pronouncements about rehabilitation without having the slightest clue about what really goes on in the nick. One word is mentioned in each and every sentence passed by a court, and that is "rehabilitation".

To give you an idea of how out of touch everyone in society is when it comes to rehabilitation you need look no further then an interview conducted on Melbourne talkback radio about eighteen months age with the then premier of Victoria, Steve Bracks. Bracks was being asked about rehab in jail and he was waffling on about what a terrific job the prison system was doing in that department. I couldn't believe my ears because a few weeks before this interview three significant incidents occurred which flew directly in the face of this proposition.

The first had been the release of convicted cop killer Peter Read in a blaze of publicity; within weeks Read was back inside, charged with a number of serious armed robberies. The second was Dane Sweetman, the neo-Nazi axe murderer. Sweetman was released, again in a blaze of publicity, and within a couple of weeks he was in trouble for fighting in a pub and being drunk. The third and easily the best is Craig Bradley (not the footballer). Craig went to jail without a drug problem and managed to acquire a raging heroin habit in jail. His habit became so bad that Craig placed himself in the drug unit and underwent detox treatment. Bradley was ultimately paroled on the basis of his rehabilitation and released. This effort begs the question of how he acquired a habit in jail, but that's another story. Craig was released and promptly shot a policeman.

What a ripping effort in the rehab department Steve.

If the premier of this state does not know these things then he should. Is the Government fair dinkum about making society better for all (not just the well healed) by providing real and effective rehabilitation and education to those locked up or are we to see more of the same... mere warehousing of blokes for the term of their sentence and then turned out on to the streets bereft of hope only to re-offend?

In June 2005 (I can't remember the exact day), at about five o'clock one evening, I heard "Fraser, officers' station!" I thought to myself, What now? I wandered over to the officers' station to be greeted unusually by the officer coming from there saying to me, "The Homicide Squad are on the phone. Do you want to talk to them?" I replied "Yes." I spoke to the Homicide Squad and had my assumption confirmed that they were ringing me about Peter Dupas, the serial killer I had worked with in the garden at Port Phillip.

The police had reinvestigated the Helvagis murder and had been informed that I had been a gardener at Port Phillip with Dupas. Maybe Dupas had spoken to me about this crime. It was nothing more than a hunch by the coppers but it was certainly worth asking me the question. Senior Detective

Paul Scarlett of the Homicide Squad rang me to see firstly, if I knew anything and secondly, whether I would talk to them. As it turns out Dupas had made a number of voluntary admissions to me about the killing of Mersina Helvagis and how he carried out that awful crime and, yes, I was prepared to assist the police. I agreed to talk to them and they were there the next morning, early on let-out. The deal thrashed out by the police and me was that I was to be released one year early if I would testify against Dupas. This was a fairly complicated procedure and David Grace QC, who had appeared in my appeal and had done such a wonderful job, again agreed to act on my behalf and for that I will be eternally grateful.

The police were very keen for me to be released because I had said to the Homicide Squad that there was not a hope in hell of me giving any evidence while I was in custody. It would be tantamount to signing my own death warrant. I made statements to the police on the understanding I would be released but I would not formalise those statements, namely swear to the contents, until such time as I had been released.

The Homicide Squad became frustrated when Paul Coughlin, the Victorian Director of Public Prosecutions, sat on that application from June 2005 until September 2006, when I was released a measly two months early. Never let it be said I've been given too many favours along the line in this case.

The homicide squad and the DPP were understandably anxious about my safety and as a result my release was to be what is known as a "controlled extraction". A controlled extraction means that, in theory, what was to happen was that the parole papers were to be faxed through to the jail to the intelligence section. Intel (as it is known) was run by Ms Kaye who was the only person at Fulham who did her job properly. The intel officer would come and collect me from work, march me to my room, have me pack up and I would be out the door. No such luck.

I was advised by David Grace on the night of Thursday 7 September 2006 that I was to be released on Monday 11 September and that it would be a "controlled extraction". Not likely. The next day being the Friday, I was called to the shift office, which is essentially where the jail is run from during the day and is right in the middle of the hub of the jail. As I was walking to the shift office, a number of crooks said to me, "Congratulations, you're going home on Monday." I was shocked because nobody was supposed to know.

I went into the shift office where an officer stood in front of a number of officers and crooks and read my parole papers to me. I pulled him aside and said that this was not the way it was supposed to be and that Kaye knew all about what was going on: my release was supposed to be a controlled extraction. The officer said, "Bad luck. This is the way it's being done" and continued to read the documents. I signed my parole papers and was told I would be released on Monday morning.

For the remainder of Friday, all of Saturday and most of Sunday I was left to my own devices to pack up and continue my existence around the jail. Everybody knew that I was going home but did not know why. My story was that I had been granted a petition of mercy because of the length of my sentence. Everybody accepted the story, luckily for me.

If, during that time from Friday afternoon to Sunday afternoon, the slightest whisper had got out that I was giving Crown evidence, I would have been dead. Fulham Correctional Centre deliberately exposed me to an unacceptable level of risk of death or injury by their negligence.

About lunchtime on Sunday the 10th Mr Walker came to me and said, "We are going to slot you [put me in solitary] until tomorrow, as you are in danger." I exploded and said to him that this was a complete and utter joke. I explained to him that it was supposed to be a controlled extraction, that Kaye knew all about it and that she was the only one who had acted even remotely professionally in this matter. Kaye was the only one I trusted. Walker repeated, "You are in danger and we are going to slot you." I said, "If that's the case, why wasn't I slotted on Friday?" To which Walker, surprisingly, stated, "I didn't know."

I had nothing left to lose. I lent over the table and said, "That is a bloody joke. You are supposed to know. You are paid to know, that is your job and I am not going to the slot." He said, "If you don't pack up your cell and go to the slot, we'll drag you there." For the first time in my entire incarceration, I became involved in some shouting and disagreement. Finally I was taken under protest to the hospital, which is next to the slot. I was placed in a single room, which may as well have been the slot because I was locked in and not allowed any communication with anybody. I was supposed to have been released at 6.30 am but once placed in the hospital cell I was advised that I was going to be released at 4.45 am in order to avoid any media that may have got wind of my release. No opportunity to tell whoever was coming to collect me. Luckily the friend who came to collect me arrived early and had been waiting for some time when I was released.

I was placed in the hospital cell and the door was locked. Dinner time came and went. I asked for dinner. I was told I would get it when they were ready: I am still waiting. I then buzzed the hospital again later in the evening and asked for a cup of tea. I was told I would get one when they were ready: I am still waiting.

Needless to say, this was a particularly exciting time for me but my excitement was mixed with apprehension and, I must say, some fear. After four years and ten months of being told when to get up, when to go to bed, when to stand by your open cell door for muster, it was all over and in a few hours I would be a free man, subject of course to my parole conditions. Notwithstanding my best efforts, looking back I realise I had to some small degree become institutionalised and life on the "outside" presented some consternation.

I did not sleep a wink that night.

At about 4 am four screws attended the hospital to escort me to property for release. I was like a cat on hot bricks but tried to keep it together. We went to property, where I was subjected to one final shit-canning by the screws. I had become used to this sort of belittling. Only a few weeks before my release, I was in the kitchen talking to the screws when they began to bag me gratuitously for some time, saying I was a fucking failure, I had fucked my life, I was a junkie, I had nothing to go home to and I would probably be back because I would get into the drugs again. Nothing like a bit of positive reinforcement to make you feel good!

I held my tongue and merely stood by while all of my possessions were checked. My money was worked out. It was given to me and I had to sign for it. Nobody gave me a hand with anything. I packed everything onto a trolley and, with that, I was unceremoniously marched out the door.

I had often pictured this moment in my mind's eye and now it had arrived. I felt a bit bewildered as I heard the prison door slam behind me. I was "out" after a long and difficult time. I was walked to the car park where my friend's car was waiting.

You might think that, after four years and tenth months, something pleasant might be said to you on departure. No such luck. Instead the inevitable jail farewell was delivered by the screws: "Fuck off!"

With that, my jail sentence was complete.

This was my day out. I stood there for a moment, rather stunned, half expecting to be grabbed and dragged back into jail. For someone who had been very confident in his previous life I was now feeling rather vulnerable. Jail had destabilised me to a huge degree and I am no longer the "rush in where angels fear to tread" type of fool that I was previously.

I walked unsteadily to the car, jumped in, and drove out of Fulham and out of the prison system.

It had been quite an odyssey but I had survived.

Omar Khayyam said, "The past we know, the future is to hand!"